BRITISH

HOME SWEET HOME

BRITAIN'S WAY OF LIFE PAST AND PRESENT

HOME SWEET HOME

A nostalgic look at domestic duties since 1945

Maggie Brogan

· MEMOIRS OF THE 20TH CENTURY ·
from
The NOSTALGIA Collection

First published in November 1999

British Library Cataloguing in Publication Data

A catalogue record for this book is available from the British Library.

ISBN 1 85895 118 6

Past & Present Publishing Ltd
The Trundle
Ringstead Road
Great Addington
Kettering
Northants
NN14 4BW

Tel/Fax: 01536 330588
e-mail: sales@slinkp-p.demon.co.uk

Printed and bound in Great Britain

Illustrations credited to 'Good Housekeeping' appear by courtesy of *Good Housekeeping* magazine © National Magazine Company.

ACKNOWLEDGEMENTS

Many people helped in the preparation of this book, and I would like to thank the following individuals who contributed their time and memories:

Margaret Adams, Bristol; Edna Archer, Keynsham, Bristol; Helen Biggs, Buckinghamshire; Brian Biles, Bristol; Monica Bourke, Bristol; Terry Brogan, Fareham, Hants; Rosie Dunn, Okehampton, Devon; Diana Faulder, Bath; Valerie Frost, Bournemouth; the Home Economics staff at Gordano School, Portishead, Bristol; Tom and Pat Hally, Bristol; Pauline Harding, Croydon, Surrey; Mary Holbrook, Bristol; Christine Hughes, Bristol; members of the Ladies Wednesday Club, Brislington Community Centre, Bristol; Sarah Levitt, London; Joan Lynes, Bristol; Christine Morgan, Narberth, Dyfed; Mike Pegler, Fareham, Hants; Dave and Marge Southall, Yate, Bristol; and Phyllis Wadsworth, Totnes, Devon.

I am also very grateful for the assistance given by the following companies and organisations:

Addis Ltd; BOSS Office Services, Bristol; Dylon International Ltd; Formica Ltd; Hoover Ltd; Imperial War Museum; Kenwood Ltd; Lever Bros, Port Sunlight; Gordon Stephenson, archivist, Reckitt & Colman Products Ltd; Stella Mitchell, Rejectamenta, Chichester, West Sussex; Singer UK Ltd; Peter Lamb, South Western Electricity Historical Society; and the SPA Partnership Ltd (MFI, Hygena and Schreiber kitchens).

BIBLIOGRAPHY

The Story of Belling 1912-1962
Davidson, Caroline *A Woman's Work Is Never Done*
Fifty Years of Change, The Bird's Eye View, 1938-1988
Flavel, Sidney & Co Ltd *Cooking the Flavel Way* (c1963)
Good Housekeeping Institute, for the Gas Council
   The Happy Home (c1947)
   The Book of Good Housekeeping (c1947)

Yarwood, Doreen *The British Kitchen*
Good Housekeeping magazines, 1952-60
Ideal Home, 1956 and 1962
National and local newspapers of the 1960s and 1970s

CONTENTS

CONVERSION TABLE

When one looks back a few decades at the prices of things, it's easy to think that just because everything cost less then, it was cheaper than it is today - but *in real terms*, of course, many things are in fact *cheaper* now, relative to our disposable income. The accompanying table shows how average wages and the prices of several staple products have changed over the decades. It is of necessity only a rough, 'round figures' guide, but it is interesting to see that while a Mars bar has gone up 10 times and a pint of bitter 20 times, wages have gone up some 36 times! The earlier figures have been converted to the nearest decimal equivalent to make the comparison easier.

	1950	1960	1970	1980	1990
Average weekly wage	£7.29	£14.10	£25.90	£109.50	£263.10
Pint of milk	2p	3p	5p	16½p	32p
Pint of bitter	5p	6p	24p	35½p	£1
Average white loaf	2½p	5p	11p	34p	53p
Mars bar	2p	2½p	3p	14p	21p

£sd/decimal conversion

2½ old pennies (d) = 1 new penny (p)

6d = 2½p

1 shilling (s) = 5p

2s 6d = 12½p

10 shillings = 50p

20 shillings = £1

Thus 22s 6d is the equivalent of £1 2s 6d, or £1 12½p.

Further price comparisons can be found on page 18.

INTRODUCTION

I considered the idea of writing a book on 50 years of housekeeping with a brain like sodden cabbage. How could I ever find enough to say about cooking, cleaning and washing to fill a book? Psychologists reckon that the brain works like a computer, probing the depths of memory. In my case it was a very slow computer - 50 years takes a lot of searching!

The 1940s are hazy. I was clothed and fed and my home was cleaned, but I was too young to notice how. All I can recall are small details like shopping with mother, ration books and penny chews.

I have fond, comfortable recollections of the 1950s, when people never locked doors and words like repossession, negative equity, redundancy and debt didn't dominate national news. It was a gentle age of seaside holidays, simple pleasures and bottles of Tizer. And, oh the envy when a friend's parents installed television, the first in the road. Friday evenings saw their living room crammed with teenage girls - including me - drooling over Hollywood heart-throb Ed 'Kookie' Burns in *77 Sunset Strip*. We drank coffee, daringly smoked the odd Craven 'A' and dreamed of marrying a film star and living in California. We never did!

Then came the Swinging Sixties. Good grief, are they really history? Memories are now so vivid that my computer-brain has moved into overdrive. That first stab of independence; moving to London - sharing a spartan flat, cooking on a gas ring and spending Saturday nights at the then revolutionary launderette. In the 1960s London was a great place to be young, and I walked the streets at midnight without fear.

But back to the book. The subject was becoming fun and my research led me ever forward. I bounced ideas around with friends, contacted long-lost relatives, interrogated everyone I met and even placed an advertisement in the local paper. I am grateful to all who replied, including members of a pensioners' club in whose lively and enthusiastic company I spent an afternoon.

I became obsessed with the domestic drama unleashed by ordinary people - strangers, in fact - who willingly shared their memories of a way of life in post-war Britain that I neither remembered nor had experienced. The more I probed the subject, the more I came up with, quickly realising that, far from worrying about having enough material, I'd be hard pressed to fit it all into one book!

So what are the changes that have transformed household management in the past five decades? A friend recently confided that she was thrown into a state of near panic when her washing machine or dishwasher broke down. Most of us are guilty of the same sense of powerlessness - literally! 'How are we going to manage?' we wail, until someone who is even older than us says, 'You'll have to do it all by hand. When I was your age. . .'

Yet that same friend admitted to deriving great pleasure from ironing linen, from lovingly polishing an old table and from lighting a real fire. Such things, she said, shine like good deeds in a naughty world. She likes doing these chores because she doesn't have to do them. Social attitudes, modern materials and domestic appliances have offered choice, and that makes all the difference.

Cooking, cleaning and washing are so much part of our everyday lives that we are almost unaware of the changes that have taken place over the last 50 years. Yet we can learn so much from the housewife's lot. What did she wear? How did she think? What were her aspirations? How was she regarded by society? How was she affected by government legislation? What transformed her life? In short, almost our entire social history can be traced through housekeeping. Each generation has realised with relief that their lot is easier than that of their mothers. Yet when reflecting on all our yesterdays, most people's reaction is to say 'Things were better then'. But is it because, in retrospect, we only remember the good times?

Certainly theft was not a cure for poverty: 'mug' was something you drank from, and £600 would buy a house, roughly the same price as today's average washing machine.

Over the past 50 years - history to some and gin-clear to others - every aspect of housekeeping has been revolutionised. This was mainly due to two factors. The first was the technological advancement of labour-saving appliances for which America takes much of the credit. The second was the huge social change that shaped women's attitude to domesticity.

The seeds germinated after the Second World War when few women chose to return to the confines of domestic service. More freedom was offered through jobs in factories, shops and offices, and they could earn better money too. Middle class housewives found themselves servantless and were forced to become their own chief cook and bottle-washer.

7

... the theme is power

Electric power—to light your leisure and to warm your ease, to cook, to clean, to preserve, to bring you music and the moving pageant of the world. Power—with economy and efficiency—in a hundred products of G.E.C.

Electric power—to run railways and light cities, to equip airports and turn the wheels of industry. Power from vast capital plant made by G.E.C.

Electric power—to carry Britain's reputation to the world's end and keep our country prosperous in the new Elizabethan age.

THE **GENERAL ELECTRIC** CO. LTD.

One of Great Britain's great companies

Electricity will 'carry Britain's reputation to the world's end and keep our country prosperous in the new Elizabethan age'. A GEC advert from about 1953. *Rejectamenta*

POWER TO THE PEOPLE

Electricity has probably done more to change our lives in the last 50 years than any other single factor. Yet in spite of publicity drives and low-cost offers to bring power into people's homes, many stuck steadfastly to gas - electricity was a newfangled idea and would never catch on!

Most domestic appliances with which we are familiar today owe their origins to turn-of-the-century engineers and inventors. Without those innovative pioneers we would still be rubbing on washboards and hand-turning mangles.

Although 1946 statistics show that 86 per cent of households were wired for electricity, this was not to the standard that we know today. It was quite common for people to install lighting only - two lights upstairs and two down. Those more adventurous souls who opted for power points also tended to err on the side of caution. 'We'll have one in the living room and one in the kitchen. What on earth do we want sockets in the bedrooms for?' was a common statement.

Brian Biles of Bristol remembers sharing a light bulb with the occupants of the bedroom next to his when he was evacuated to Devon during the war. 'There was a hole cut in the wall between the two rooms with a single light bulb fitted into the gap,' he explains.

Small appliances such as irons, radios, kettles and fires were designed with long leads for plugging

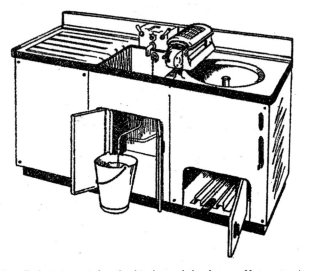

'An all-electric unit for the kitchen of the future. Hot water is provided from a tank under the draining board, and the washing machine in on the right. Note the little store cupboard for the detachable wringer and the convenient arrangements for filling a bucket without too much lifting.' Circa 1947. *Good Housekeeping*

into ceiling light sockets. Few people owned a vacuum cleaner or fridge, fewer still invested in a washing machine or dishwasher, and microwaves were the stuff of science fiction.

• It is hard to believe that within the living memory of many, electricity was such a novelty that light bulbs were left exposed as a proud statement of installing the very latest technology!

• Experiments to develop electric irons began in the latter part of the 19th century. Indeed, an example made in 1889 exploded, killing its inventor.

• In 1912, Charles Belling invented a revolutionary water heater that boiled 12 pints of water in one minute. 'There was only one snag,' he later admitted. 'It took a 10-kilowatt load, which in those days dimmed the lights for miles around.'

• American experiments with 'pop-up' toasters proved a little too enthusiastic. Toast tended to catch fire then shoot 6 feet through the air.

• Instructions accompanying early electric fires carried the warning 'Do not use a poker'.

• Notices in hotels stated: 'This room is equipped with electric light. Do not attempt to light with a match.'

• Control boxes on early electric cookers often gave off sparks, flashes and a sinister humming.

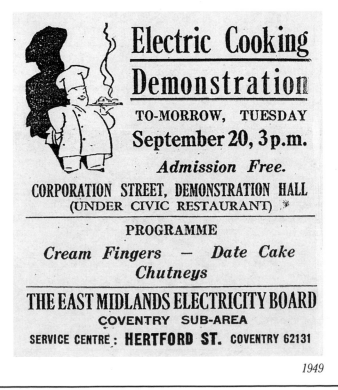

Manufacturers, foreseeing a potentially huge buying public, rose to the challenge. Domestic aids flooded the market. But anything new and revolutionary is initially expensive, and many appliances were slow to filter through a class-ridden society. Indeed, some never reached the less well-off at all.

In today's so-called affluent society, to have or have not is likely to be a decision based on 'Do I really want it?' rather than 'Can I afford it?'. Although the cost of living rises year by year, domestic appliances have, in real terms, become less expensive as the shift from luxury to necessity has gradually taken place. For example, in 1946 only 2 per cent of households owned a powered washing machine; in 1994 the figure was 91 per cent.

During the Second World War the famous 'Dig For Victory' campaign encouraged the entire population to grow its own food. By 1943 there were almost one and a half million allotment holders, half of whom were women. Vegetable gardens camouflaged air-raid shelters, which led people to comment that they were more at risk from falling marrows than enemy bombs! Innovation flourished among rich and poor and young and old. Stately homes turned tennis courts and rose beds into vegetable plots.

The Ministry of Food bombarded women with suggestions of how to feed the family for days on a single pig's head, and how to glean food from hedgerows. Mashed potato and melted margarine became a butter substitute, and potatoes were used in everything from Christmas cakes to 'fruit' flans. Sandwiches were filled with nasturtium leaves, grated beetroot or rhubarb and marrow jam. I always enjoyed mother's wartime sandwiches; it was years later that I discovered the filling was black pepper!

By 1940 everyone had registered for ration books. With each person allocated a shillings-worth of meat, tuppenceworth of corned beef and one egg per week, it was common for women to do without themselves to ensure their husbands and children were well fed.

'Housewives always looked after the breadwinner,' explains Brian Biles. 'My father cycled six miles to work and mother made sure he ate a cooked breakfast each morning. I was 14 at the time and worked as a grocer's delivery boy. Rations for a family of four packed into a box just 15 by 12 inches and cost about £1.

'Families where the mothers were competent cooks fared well because they were brilliant at making something out of nothing. Others hadn't a clue and went through their rations in no time. Tinned salmon, which was fairly plentiful, was a popular choice for Sunday tea, and it would be stretched to serve four.'

Fresh fish was not rationed, and fish and chip shops stayed open during the war. Many people recall living on a threepenny piece of fish and tuppence-worth of chips. The school meals scheme also started, which gave mothers the chance to work; a labour directive campaign sent young, fit women to firms that needed them most.

A bartering economy developed, with egg and clothing coupons hot property on the black market.

Monica Bourke's father worked for Imperial Tobacco. 'Our local butcher was a chain smoker,' she recalls, 'so my father bribed him with cigarettes. Good stuff was kept under the counter - sausages, kidneys and liver, although not rationed, were scarce, and it was a treat to have them.'

Children were quick to realise a solution to sweet rationing, which continued until 1953. 'We'd buy medicinal liquorice and Zubes from chemist shops,' remembers one, 'and if we were lucky, sticks of diabetic barley sugar. I was evacuated to Frome in Somerset and one weekend on my return to London I ate a whole jar of Horlicks tablets. I felt really sick, but I didn't dare tell my parents why I couldn't eat tea!'

If people thought wartime food shortages were bad, worse was yet to follow. Wartime bread, although grey and unappetising, was never rationed, but in 1946 the Government announced shortages of flour due to a world crop failure. There was a public outcry. Where housewives had looked forward to a time of plenty when the war ended, they now faced further cuts, even lower rations and long queues to buy what little produce was available.

'If you saw a queue you just joined it because you never knew what you might be missing,' remembers Pauline Harding. 'I almost lived on roast pigeon and stuffed rabbit because they were cheap and plentiful, if you knew the right person!'

Nora Whiting, who was a child at the time, recalls her local church providing a bowl of stew for poor families at three-farthings per quart.

Keeping warm was another problem, as Monica Bourke explains. 'Coal was rationed per household regardless of the size of your house. It was enough for one meagre fire each day. We had an Ideal boiler, which burst in the cold winter of 1947. We waited six weeks for a Government permit before my father was allowed to replace it. Mother had a tough time with three children in the family. A couple of years later we applied to have electricity installed. We were allowed just five lights and one power point!'

Self-sufficiency became even more important in post-war years, and it was not just country folk who provided much of their own food. Rosie Dunn recalls her childhood in suburban Surrey.

'I was one of five children, and our parents were teachers,' she says. 'We were all expected to help dig potatoes, shell peas and collect eggs, often before walking to school. We had a cow called Avis, which the older children milked twice a day. Milk was made into butter and cream, then the residue was fed to our two pigs.

'Roast chicken was always on the menu for Sunday lunch. I can see my father now, running round the garden calling to my mother, "How many do you want, Lillian?" Then it was the job of us children to pluck and clean the birds ready for cooking.

'There's a whole generation today who believe that peas are made by Birds Eye and who have never known anything but supermarket chickens neatly cleaned and trussed on polystyrene trays.'

RATIONING

During the Second World War and for several years afterwards, food, petrol, clothing and soap were rationed. During the 14 years of shortages (1940-54) ration amounts fluctuated; for example, cheese ranged from 1 oz per week in 1941 to 8 oz in 1942, then dropped again to 3 oz in 1943. Meat was the last product to come off ration in 1954. The following table gives some ration examples.

Bacon and ham	4 oz per week
Meat	1s 2d worth (about 8 oz) per week
Cheese	1 oz per week
Butter	4 oz per week
Sugar	8 oz per week
Tea	2 oz per week
Jam, syrup, marmalade and treacle	8 oz per month
Cooking fat	2 oz per week
Chocolate and sweets	8 oz per month
Milk	2 pints per week
Whole eggs	1 egg per week
Oranges	4 lb per year
Clothing	48 coupons per year (16 coupons bought an adult overcoat, 8 a skirt and 2 a pair of stockings)

Today, more than ever before, Refrigeration is a necessity

If rationed food goes bad it cannot be replaced. In recognition of this fact the Government installed 80,000 'built-in' Electrolux Gas Refrigerators in temporary "Prefabs". Many Local Authorities followed this lead when planning their Permanent Housing Schemes.

Gas operated Electrolux Refrigerators easily fit into any kitchen plan. They can be built into modern kitchen furniture at any height. The only moving part of an Electrolux Refrigerator is its door! There is no machinery. This means freedom from vibration, low maintenance cost, dependability and absolute *Silence* at all times.

Electrolux Ltd. are the originators of the continuous Absorption Process which accounts for the permanent SILENCE of Electrolux Refrigerators. Only Electrolux Cabinets contain the Silent Electrolux Cooling Unit.

BUILT-IN Silent Electrolux REFRIGERATORS
Operated by Gas

ELECTROLUX LIMITED, LUTON, BEDS.   Head Office, 153/5, REGENT STREET, LONDON, W.1.

Electrolux

In post-war Britain there was a chronic shortage of fuel and raw materials - and therefore consumer goods. The Government, desperate for money, urged manufacturers into a big export drive. Many advertisements carried warnings of long waiting lists.

'There was little or no choice,' recalls Phyllis Wadsworth. 'If for example you wanted a carpet, you'd put your name down at the store. When notification came that one had arrived, you didn't ask the size, colour or price, you just said yes or no.'

In spite of the doom and gloom, manufacturers were encouraging housewives to look forward to a brighter future. Easier-to-work-in kitchens, electrical gadgets that would chop, mince, beat, cream and grind, and more efficient cleaning products were all aimed to remove the drudgery from housework.

GLOW
home with
BOVRIL

Long queues . . . wet streets . . . cold winds—you take them all in your stride when you're glowing cheerfully after your hot Bovril. Bovril is concentrated beefy goodness . . . use it to put beef into meatless meals, too.

The concentrated goodness of Beef

Bovril helps your digestion to get *all* the goodness out of your food and builds up reserves to resist winter ills. Bovril stimulates your appetite and your sense of taste.

G.H. 1952

"When it's NEW ZEALAND it's Good"

It may not always be available on request under present conditions, but an ever-increasing production hastens the day when the Housewife can make her choice

NEW ZEALAND LAMB *The Best in the World*

Left and above Queues and shortages reflected in two 1952 advertisements.

Right and below Advertisements from 1952 for Electrolux and Bendix warning of long waits for delivery.

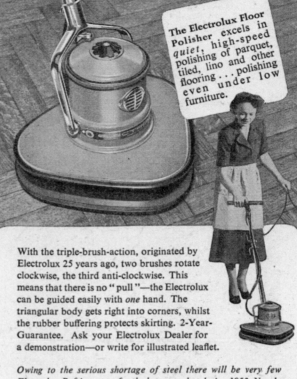

The Electrolux Floor Polisher excels in *quiet*, high-speed polishing of parquet, tiled, lino and other flooring... polishing even under low furniture.

With the triple-brush-action, originated by Electrolux 25 years ago, two brushes rotate clockwise, the third anti-clockwise. This means that there is no "pull"—the Electrolux can be guided easily with *one* hand. The triangular body gets right into corners, whilst the rubber buffering protects skirting. 2-Year-Guarantee. Ask your Electrolux Dealer for a demonstration—or write for illustrated leaflet.

Owing to the serious shortage of steel there will be very few Electrolux Refrigerators for the home market during 1952. Nearly all the output must go abroad to meet the urgent need for exports.

How does the Electrolux Cleaner remove *all* the dust and grit? Only by suction. But then, Electrolux *excels* in deep, penetrating suction... without shock or wear to the finest fabric. All tools for floor-to-ceiling cleaning—and a sprayer—without extra cost. H.P. Terms available. 2-Year-Guarantee.

Electrolux *Excels...*

By Appointment Refrigerator Makers to the late King George VI

By Appointment Suction Cleaner and Refrigerator Manufacturers to H.M. Queen Mary

Electrolux Ltd., 153/5 Regent Street, London, W.1.

The Reward of Patience

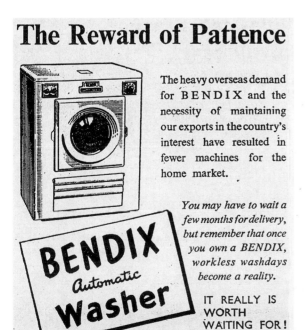

The heavy overseas demand for BENDIX and the necessity of maintaining our exports in the country's interest have resulted in fewer machines for the home market.

You may have to wait a few months for delivery, but remember that once you own a BENDIX, workless washdays become a reality.

IT REALLY IS WORTH WAITING FOR!

BENDIX *Automatic* **Washer**

Full particulars from:

BENDIX HOME APPLIANCES LTD., DEPT. J, ALBION WORKS, KINGSBURY RD., BIRMINGHAM, 24.

The Electrolux Cleaner excels in suction power. Yet it's so *quiet* that one can always hear the doorbell... the telephone.

Electrolux

that magic touch with a *Kenwood* Chef

and its 14 wonderful attachments

31 GNS.
for the standard pack—including K-beater, dough hook, whisk, mixing bowl, spatula, dust cover and instruction and recipe book

Left This Kenwood Chef was a hefty 31 guineas (£32 11s) in the 1950s; a similar modern food processor is less than three times that price today, 40 years later! *Kenwood Ltd*

Above The new electric age, 1953: housewives in adverts stood beside new gas and electric cookers that were stuffed full of food, as though the appliance had done all the preparation too.

Right and below Floor mops promised no more aching backs or sore knees, and cleaning materials boasted hours of work saved.

Reckitt & Colman Products Ltd

For most women housekeeping was a full-time job. They got married and gave up work to look after their husbands and home: men were the breadwinners and women kept house. Straight and simple. If he was seen to wash dishes he was considered hen-pecked, and there was a certain shame among some classes if married women went out to work.

The media reflected this social attitude by showing women in domestic situations. A magazine feature of 1953 gives illustrated instructions for ironing a man's shirt. It also states: 'There is a tremendous satisfaction in the picture of a full line of drying clothes, white as the driven snow, happily billowing in a gentle breeze on a sunny day.' Hardly the stuff you'd read in a modern edition of *Cosmo*!

It was the era of sexism in its extreme. Advertisements showed happy women, usually glamorously dressed and wearing a variety of frilly aprons, offering their man all manner of food and drink. Cooking was as important as the act of love itself. A woman's place was in the home and she was proud to be there. Most were financially dependent on their husbands and it was to the man of the house that advertisements for the newly arrived domestic appliances were aimed.

In spite of a booming white goods industry in the 1950s, the majority of homes were devoid of labour-saving equipment. Yet a high standard of housekeeping was expected. It was quite normal for women to devote

Left Looking after 'that man of yours' in 1953! *Reckitt & Colman Products Ltd*

Below and right Advertisements showed happy women, usually glamorously dressed and wearing a variety of frilly aprons, offering their man all manner of food and drink.

Reward for a good cook!

Make your new cooker an *electric* one— and give yourself a reward for years of delicious cooking. Or, if you're a young housewife, start off with all the advantages of electricity. Fortunately there's no trouble about installation or running costs – simplicity and economy are two of the highlights of electric cooking.

It's so easy–it's like cheating! Right from the beginning the young housewife finds she can bake, when her cooker's electric! There are no draughts to flatten her cake just as it's nicely rising, or to burn it on one side. And joints stay juicy and hardly shrink at all.

It's so clean, you won't know your kitchen! Until you install an electric cooker you won't know how much difference it makes to the cleanliness of your kitchen. But you'll soon notice that you're washing the curtains much less often, and all the paint stays brighter.

It's so clever – it can switch itself on! If you get one of the new auto-time models you can set it to switch itself on, cook the meal and switch itself off–all while you're out of the house!

Your Electricity Service Centre is the place to see all the latest models and hear about the very easy hire purchase terms.

Cooking... get up to date   go electric!

Issued by the Electrical Development Association

between 12 and 14 hours a day to domestic duties. They seldom, if ever, had a completely free day in the week. Household management tomes of the time advised housewives to rise early in order to complete all the cleaning, cooking, washing and sewing that was expected of them.

One daughter recalls her childhood memories in the 1950s. 'My father had a good job and was never out of work. We enjoyed a comfortable standard of living, although mother was very frugal and kept to a stringent budget. He was a traditionalist and refused to let my mother get a job, which is what she wanted. No wife of his was going out to work, he said.

'There were only three of us in the family, so mother must have had time on her hands. Yet my recollections are that from dawn to dusk she was on the go. It was as though she felt guilty of a duty neglected if she wasn't seen to be scrubbing, washing and cooking and generally waiting on my father hand and foot.

'Saturdays were usually spent baking - buns, cakes, pies, that sort of thing - to tide us over the following week. I never remember her meeting friends or even reading a book. She was always saying that she didn't have time, although she admits now, like other women of her era, that she was a slave to her home.

'There was a certain snobbery about what you ate,

Left Despite adverts like this, the majority of 1950s homes were devoid of labour-saving equipment. *South Western Electricity Historical Society*

THOSE WERE THE DAYS. . .

This table compares typical costs between the beginning of the 1960s and 1996. However, remember also to compare average incomes for the two periods - see page 5.

		1996
Television licence (1962)	£4 0s 0d	£89.50
Bottle of whisky (1960)	£1 12s 6d	£11.79
Annual subscription to *Which* magazine (1961)	£1 0s 0d	£59
Annual RAC membership (1961)	£2 2s 0d	£69
Term's fees at girls' private school (1959)	£26 15s 2d	£1,425
School blazer (1962)	£9 19s 6d	£51
One cwt coal (1961)	9s 4d	£7
Driving licence (1960)	15s 0d	£21
Bifocal glasses (1960)	£9 5s 0d	£70-£125
		1996
Set of dentures (1960)	£4 5s 0d	£100 (NHS), £400 (private)
Good quality man's suit (1960)	£28 0s 0d	£300
Record player (1961)	£21 6s 11d	£300
Cheapest ticket for Wembley Cup Final (1960)	3s 6d	£25
Cost of three-bed semi in South of England (1966)	£2,800	£86,000
Annual rates and water charges on a four-bed detached bungalow (1960)	£54 1s 6d	£1,355
Telephone line rental (1961)	£3 10s 0d	£24.78 (inc VAT)

maybe a reaction against wartime food shortages. My father considered it shameful if you couldn't afford meat. He would have grumbled for weeks if mother had served up something like aubergine gratin - he'd have asked where the main course was!

'And he'd never have anything but butter on the table. Margarine was for the poor, he said. No one had heard about the ravages of red meat and cholesterol in those days.'

A friend recalls: 'We lived in a rather poor area and once a neighbour popped in while we were eating. Mother felt guilty about being able to afford fish, when all around us couldn't, so she said the cat had found it. We children kept a straight face - you wouldn't have dared to do anything else in those days.'

Then the 'Swinging Sixties' erupted. The young craved freedom. Girls had been educated to the same level as boys and they wanted fun - a New World that wasn't restricted by an elbows-off-the-table-don't-dare-leave-anything-on-your-plate regime. Out went the assumption that a woman's place was in the home.

This was the era when coffee bars, Coca-Cola and Craven 'A' satisfied the ambition for a good night out. Bright young things flocked to Benidorm instead of Blackpool, taking their skin-tight jeans, stiletto heels and winklepicker shoes with them.

Yes, young women were demanding more from life than domestic chains. They weren't so interested in burning their bras as burying their frilly aprons, and advertising copywriters were quick to respond, as the accompanying examples show.

It was suddenly acceptable to continue working after marriage and daringly chic to live with a member of the opposite sex before marriage. Women spent their own money on labour-saving devices to allow themselves more leisure. With men no longer the sole earners, the balance of power within the family began to shift and the traditional roles of men and women began to crumble.

The 1970s, born under the real threat of nuclear war, brought a new awareness that life and the planet were valuable commodities. As daft as it sounds now, a Government leaflet dropped through our letter-boxes advising us how to turn our understairs cupboard into a nuclear-free zone.

While men grew their hair, women started worrying about their children's future, the chemicals in food and whether their Sunday roast had enjoyed a natural life. The press went into lurid detail about battery hens, veal production and hormone-injected meat, while the National Childbirth extolled the virtues of breast-feeding.

Droves of young professionals, who had never grown a carrot in their lives, took off to far-flung corners of the UK in search of the Good Life. It was a time of unrest and instability. The era brought miners' strikes, postal strikes, refuse collectors' strikes, telephone operators' go-slow, the threat of petrol

TO WASHING MACHINE OWNERS

NEW LIQUID BLUE MAKES WHITES BRIGHT IN EVERY LIGHT

BY DAY **BY NIGHT**

Many washing powders make whites whiter — in daylight and some artificial lights. Only Reckitt's New Liquid Blue gives you true whiteness in all lights — day or night. This means you can look your very best even by artificial light; and your sheets and pillow cases can now be something to be proud of.

SPECIALLY DESIGNED FOR WASHING MACHINES
Reckitt's New Liquid Blue, specially designed for washing machines, could not be simpler to use. Just a squeeze into the wash water *(not the rinse)* and it does the work for you while you wash. There is no harsh bleach to shorten the life of fabrics in New Liquid Blue. *And* it's lavender scented.

NEW FOR ALL WASHING MACHINES

Reckitt's LIQUID BLUE

In the easy to use squeeze bottle 1/-

1962; Reckitt & Colman Products Ltd

rationing and the three-day week. Sales of candles soared as power cuts plunged the country into darkness again and again.

One young housewife of the time recalls, 'We still had the old gas lights in our turn-of-the-century house. Not only did they provide much welcome light, but the atmosphere was wonderful. Somehow the soft romantic glow toned down the harshness of the time.'

Then the Thatcherite era promised a bright dot of hope on the horizon. We were told that we could have it all if we worked hard, started our own business, bought our own home and provided our own pension and health insurance. Enter the 'yuppies' (Young Upwardly-mobile Professionals) in a whirl of BMWs and penthouse flats. Enormous salaries became a byword, house prices escalated and borrowing reached an all-time high. No one seemed to give a thought as to how they would repay the money if things went wrong. But things wouldn't go wrong, would they? We'd never had it so good.

Inspired by The Lady herself, a new breed of housewife emerged - Superwoman. She was supposed to be the perfect wife and hostess, caring mother and single-minded career woman. Those who chose to stay at home and look after their families were condescendingly referred to as 'the little woman'. To admit that you ironed shirts and cooked steak and kidney pie was a betrayal of your sex. Women flocked to evening classes to learn how to become more assertive, and newspapers carried features proclaiming '20 Ways To Reach The Top'.

Upmarket and professionally run domestic services mushroomed to meet the demands of Superwoman. For a price you could have your

c1960   'A well-bred gypsy in a long chiffon dress', c1970. *Rejectamenta*

laundry collected, ironed and returned; your dog walked and cat fed; your freezer filled; your clothes chosen; and your children cared for. Uniformed house cleaners arrived in smart sign-written vans, and finishing-school-educated Sloane Rangers took gift buying and dinner party worries off your hands.

Even women who opted to employ this new breed of servant now admit that they were riddled with guilt and tension trying to organise their housewifely duties alongside a demanding career. 'By the time I arrived at the office I felt I'd done a day's work already,' recalls one former Superwoman. Another reports, 'When I found myself pregnant I was in my early 30s and head of a personnel department. I had no intention of giving up work, but I soon found that I couldn't be three things at once - not to the standard I wanted, anyway. Neither did I have the energy to give my husband the emotional support that men seem to need. I had enough stress in my own job.'

Few made the grade; juggling supermarket and boardroom just didn't work. Criticised by childcare experts, rejected by bosses and cold-shouldered by husbands, Superwoman all but vanished like a puff of Vacfresh.

Simultaneously came the economic crunch - high interest rates, recession, repossession, bankruptcy, redundancy, unemployment, empty shops and abandoned office blocks. Those who had climbed to the top in next to no time fell twice as fast, realising that their pursuit of money and success was but a dream. It didn't matter whether you were a lawyer or a lorry driver and had given your whole life to one firm, redundancy loomed (and still does) like a spectre.

Thousands retreated from the world, licked their wounds and took stock of their lives. Repercussions of the get-rich-quick years are still being felt by families throughout the country, and today's woman is likely to make the choice between high-flier and housewife more carefully. Does she want a career and risk sacrificing motherhood, or should she give in gracefully, retire to a beamed farmhouse, change nappies and make jam?

The long road to independence is taking an unexpected turn - back up the driveway. A decade ago, liberated women would have scorned a 1957 review for a newly published Good Housekeeping book: 'Even in this age of labour shortage and high prices, home-making remains for a woman the most rewarding of all occupations.'

Today, taking an interest in one's home has never been so popular, as the number of glossy magazines devoted to the subject bear witness. Those who had their fingers burned financially in the 1980s are learning to live on a less than average salary, believing that quality of life is now more important than quantity.

Down-stepping has become the theme tune for today's man. It means trading in the three-piece suit, company car and expense account for a simpler job and a better lifestyle. Bank managers have become market gardeners and economists have become musicians. Men who once walked the corridors of power find social acceptance and therapy in cooking, and it is a fact of modern life that his wife might earn more than him, or indeed be the breadwinner. She may even choose divorce. But either way housewives have had to adapt.

Increasingly we are looking to the past for answers. There is an enormous surge towards the solid comforts of an old-fashioned way of life - self-sufficiency, candlelight, open fires, range-style cookers, deep china sinks and jam roly-poly. Even smart restaurants are now featuring traditional puddings on their menus - the type that are 'as warm and comfortable as a red flannel petticoat', as my grandmother used to say.

Life is still busy for today's housewife, but it is not because she is forced to trudge the eternal triangle of sink, cooker and table. For the many women who are content to juggle work and family, a daily cleaner or nanny is often employed, although the relationship is equal rather than the mistress-servant attitude.

Easy-care and drip-dry have put paid to piles of ironing higher than the National Debt; washing machines, fridge-freezers and microwaves are standard kitchen equipment; everything from ready-prepared meals to take-aways have removed the slog of feeding the family and, in our centrally heated age, the flickering flames of a real fire are a visual comfort rather than the sole source of warmth.

There is work involved in laying a fire, polishing old wood, ironing linen and making *boeuf en croûte*. But it's the housewife's choice. Today we have the freedom to take the romance and graciousness from the past and the labour-saving practicality from the present.

1. COUNTRY LIVING

If housekeeping was an arduous task for town dwellers, it was even worse for those who lived in the country. Christine Morgan recalls her days in Cornwall, first as a teenager on a farm, then as a young wife with a home of her own. Between 1947 and 1957, 'mod cons' meant an Acme wringer and a battery wireless!

'We moved to Red Post Farm in 1947. There was no electricity, bathroom or piped water supply. Water was pumped from the outside well, boiled up in saucepans on the coal range then tipped into a hip bath that stood by the fire. You sat in it with your knees around your neck. My parents then carried the bath outside and emptied it. Needless to say we didn't have a bath very often!

It is hard to imagine life without instant hot water at the turn of a tap. Yet visions of women queuing at standpipes, pumps and springs is not a figment of medieval history but a post-war reality. In 1951, 20 per cent of households in England and Wales were without a piped water supply. In 1947 conditions were even worse in Northern Ireland where, in parts of Ulster, 92 per cent of homes were without a supply. People drew their water from wells, either in their gardens or from a community pump which served several households.

Tom Hally recalls washing his clothes at the village pump in the 1960s after traipsing three-quarters of a mile to reach it.

'All the family were expected to carry buckets of water back to the house, which were stored on the kitchen dresser,' he explains.

Margaret Adams remembers villagers in Gloucestershire collecting water from a spring. 'On washdays, water running down the sides of the road was blue,' she says. 'After women had done their washing they just chucked the water out into the street. We were lucky. In our farmhouse we had a convenient water supply - a stone trough built into the kitchen wall, which was permanently fed from a spring in the hillside. It was still being used when we left in 1974 and may still be in use for all I know.'

Christine Morgan recalls a similar situation in 1950s Cornwall. 'There was a stone trough in the kitchen fed from a stream via a pipe. Everyone - cats, dogs and people - drew their water from it.'

Some townsfolk didn't fare much better. Pauline Harding married in 1949 and lived in suburban Bristol. 'We rented a flat above a shop and the water supply was on the ground floor only. A great part of my day was spent lugging buckets of water up the stairs.' *Pauline Harding/Tom Hally (3)*

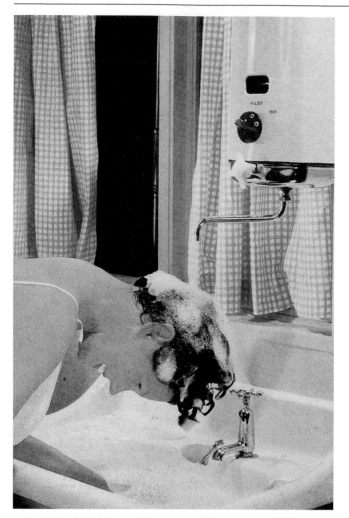

Above Rural areas also had to wait a long time for electricity. In 1948, the date of this 'past' picture, two-thirds of the South West, which stretched from Bristol to the Scilly Isles, lacked supplies. As a result few enjoyed the luxury of instant hot water to wash their hair; often the job entailed a major juggling act with a motley collection of jugs and kettles, which resulted in a flooded floor and wet sleeves.

Although Drene is a well remembered brand, there wasn't the choice of shampoos on the market. Margaret Adams recalls using a block of household soap and rainwater - her hair shone like a halo! Brenda Dix recalls her family's method. 'After mother had done the weekly wash in her boiler, she'd leave the soapy water to cool, when it set like grey junket. This is what we scooped out and boiled up to wash our hair. Soap was scarce during the war, you see, so we couldn't waste any.'

Joan Morris fared rather better. She used shampoo powder, mixed to a paste with water, then made setting lotion from an amalgam of sugar and water. When her hair was dry she rubbed it with a candle to add shine.

Today women are likely to wash their hair in the shower, or with the aid of a mixer-tap spray over the bath, or indulge in regular visits to the hairdresser. The cosmetic industry now represents a boom market, and hair preparations form a large part. An infinite variety of shampoos, conditioners, colorants, gels, mousses, shine concoctions, for both men and women, are now available. Great importance is placed on natural ingredients - today's hair preparations almost sound good enough to eat! Varieties such as Royal Jelly, Sea Kelp, Honey, Lemon and Wild Herbs jostle for the purchaser's attention. *Good Housekeeping/MB*

Below 'Water was pumped from a well in the garden,' remembers Christine Morgan, 'but I'd go to mum's for a bath so I didn't have to heat up gallons of water. Our toilet was an Elsan bucket, the contents of which were buried in the garden. As my husband was away in the Merchant Navy, I had to do the job myself.'

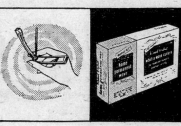
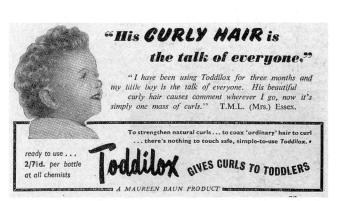
Curly hair was all the rage. As an alternative to commercially available 'home perm' kits, Joan Winscombe would wind her hair into curls, which were fixed into place with two crossed hairpins. 'As I had fair hair it dried leaving rusty brown crosses all over my head.'

Post-war mothers went to great lengths to achieve the ultimate status symbol - a Shirley Temple lookalike. It didn't matter whether their offspring were boys or girls, curls were definitely 'in'. If nature hadn't provided, there were manufacturers who could, as these c1952 adverts show.

Christine Morgan's house was lit by means of 'Tilly' or 'Aladdin' lamps, which were equal to the power of 120 candles. 'A travelling hardware man called from whom we bought wicks, mantles, paraffin and wireless batteries. These were rechargeable and big - very much like the car batteries of today.

'A grocer, fishmonger and butcher also called once a week, together with a fish and chip man; I can still remember his name - Sid Collins. Mum went to Holsworthy market on Wednesdays, which helped me with shopping because by this time I had two babies. If you wanted anything special you'd have to catch the bus to Launceston, Tavistock or Plymouth; although it's not far by today's standards, it was a major journey then and you'd be away all day.

'Obviously living on a farm we had plenty of milk, eggs and poultry. Cream was made by hand and eggs were preserved in isinglass to last us through the winter. Two pigs were killed each year, cut into joints, then salted or smoked. Great sides of bacon hung from the rafters and we just cut bits off when needed. Mum always said she had no money and that all she owned walked about on two or four legs!

'We had a small Calor gas fridge, but most food was kept in the dairy, which was very cold with a flagstone floor, stone shelves and wire mesh windows.

'In 1950 we installed a bathroom, an Aga and a generator. We suddenly had hot water and proper lights, although the generator had to be switched off at night, so we still went to bed by candle light. But to us it was like living at the Savoy! Mum burned anthracite in the Aga and logs in the fireplaces to heat other rooms. If the wind was blowing the wrong way, anthracite fumes came down the chimney into the kitchen and covered everything with black dust.

'In 1953 I married and moved to a house that again had no bathroom, electricity or piped water. I boiled the kettle on a Primus stove and cooked meals on a Rayburn, which burned coal and wood. In summer we lived on salads because it was too hot to light the Rayburn.

'Lighting was by lamps and candles, but I did have a modern wireless - an Ever Ready portable which operated on an ordinary battery, the type you buy today.'

'Washing was done by hand,' recalls Christine. 'I used an old preserving pan to boil sheets, pillowcases, towels and nappies, one item at a time - it took hours.' She also had an Acme wringer, as featured in this advert from November 1945, which was a great boon.

'I pressed the clothes with two flat irons, heated on the Rayburn. That way one was kept hot while I ironed with the other. I think they had a chromium plate that slipped on to give a smooth surface for ironing.'

26

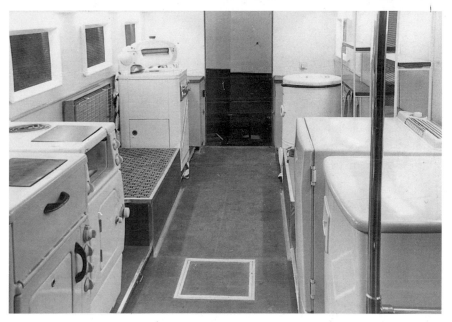

Travelling electricity and gas board showrooms visited country districts with a van full of the latest cookers and other appliances, although Christine Morgan never saw one in her area. In 1957 she moved again to a 'modern' house where there was a Calor gas cooker and a solid fuel boiler, which heated water for the bathroom, but still no electricity.

'I did the laundry in a coal-fired wash boiler that was built into a corner of the kitchen. I'd fill it from a cold water tap in the wall, but it had to be emptied by scooping out the water with a saucepan. Travelling tradesmen still called, plus the Calor gas man, coal merchant, shoe repairer and visiting library.

'When my son started school we'd walk 3 miles to the village each morning. I'd do my shopping at the local store at the same time, then I'd collect him too - that was 12 miles' walking a day.

'Life was very mundane. Most of the time I was on my own with two small children, but there was so much work involved just keeping us clean, clothed and fed that I suppose I was too busy to get lonely. Of course, looking back I wonder how on earth I put up with it.' *W. W. Winter/South Western Electricity Historical Society*

2. KITCHENS

In homes of poorer families, or those living in rural areas, change was slow in coming to post-war kitchens. Often there was no electricity and the kitchen doubled as a sitting room. Linoleum covered the floor, a 'copper' stood in the corner for wash days, and a couple of horsehair chairs flanked the hearth.

Even in new houses the kitchen was almost ignored by architects; it was the Cinderella of the home and many housewives put up with basic working conditions and a penny-pinching lifestyle. As Britain looked forward to a bright new future in post-war years, new-style furniture was needed to suit smaller rooms and a different way of life.

Experts suggested re-planning kitchens rather than purchasing indiscriminately. Providing adequate storage, minimising cleaning chores and avoiding unnecessary walking backwards and forwards were considered more important than a wealth of electrical gadgets. Housewives were keen to improve their lot and many took advantage of the modular kitchen units that were appearing on the market. These were of a standard size and could be mixed and matched in a variety of layouts. Popular arrangements included a run down one or two walls or around a corner, with appliances tacked on each end, as seen in this c1948 example. The sink, almost without exception, was positioned under the window, no doubt to remind housewives that there was life beyond the kitchen!

The post-war theory of the well-planned kitchen as a cheerful place to work is also reflected in the 1990s design illustrated here. The cabinets may be laminated, but gone is the glossy plastic uniformity and utilitarian image. Any starkness is counter-acted by the soft ivory colour, timber worktops and limed wood walls. It also incorporates modern innovations as well as some old ones. Sinks are no longer necessarily positioned under the window, although peninsula fitments have retained popularity over the last 40 years. The chimney extractor fan above the built-in cooker and hob makes a striking modern statement. *Good Housekeeping/Schreiber at MFI*

Right The completely fitted kitchen that incorporated integrated appliances and specially designed carousel fitments to utilise wasted corner space was a 1950s phenomenon, as seen in this 1956 advertisement.

Below A 1952 English Rose kitchen, which was a style leader at the time. With its clean, uncluttered lines, electrical accessories, fitted cooker and glossy red and white plastic laminated furniture, it epitomised every young wife's dream. Yet in spite of the availability of such designs, it was some years before fitted kitchens became the norm.

The 1950s were a time of fashionable domesticity and the kitchen was the heartland of family life. Men were enjoying home comforts after the rigours of war and women were content to make sure they had them. Mother's home cooking and the evening meal was the main family event of the day.

This 1956 Redwing advertisement states that the kitchen is the housewife's workroom - a kitchen, cafeteria, laundry and nursery all rolled into one. With the age of austerity fading, it was in the kitchen that the housewife spent much of her day, lovingly cooking her husband's meals and ironing his shirts.

Throughout the 1970s, kitchens remained places where work was done - washing and chopping vegetables, cooking meals, doing the laundry. Washing machines, dishwashers, microwaves, food processors and tumble dryers were installed in their thousands. Then, when there was nothing left to buy, attention focused on the kitchen itself. What had simply been the engine room of the house became the all-singing, all-dancing raison d'être of homemaking.

Kitchens were dragged and stippled, distressed and stencilled. Pretty colours were combined with natural wood, and the less it looked like a workroom the better people liked it. This 1996 Shaker-style kitchen is rather like the perfect husband - hard-working, good-looking and pleasant to be around! *Schreiber at MFI*

The 1960s kitchen flaunted technology. With a new era of affluence, more housewives could afford labour-saving gadgets and modern materials that had only been dreamed of in previous decades. The fitted kitchen had well and truly arrived, and with it came an image of a clean new world, uncluttered and uniform. Split-level cookers, corner carousel units and breakfast bars were all the rage. Ranks of glossy cupboards kept everything neatly out of sight and cleaning to a minimum. Shiny stainless steel saucepans and electrical appliances were kitchen status symbols of the age.

The young career girl of the 1960s became the wife and mother of the '70s and acres of germ-free glossy laminate were a constant reminder of what she didn't want - domesticity. The style that epitomised the dream of the 1950s and '60s was regarded as something of a nightmare, and the desire for functional fitted kitchens vanished almost overnight.

One firm that was largely responsible for changing the face of kitchens is Smallbone of Devizes, whose designs came like a breath of spring air to housewives who were weary of mass-produced plastic. Smallbone overturned the post-war design theory that the kitchen was merely a machine for cooking. The company dispensed with shiny plastic chipboard in preference to properly panelled doors in traditional woods. In the late 1970s Smallbone's kitchens evoked a simple country image with furniture made from reclaimed antique pine; the design (*below left*) was destined to become a classic. The furniture may have been just as fitted, but it cleverly disguised the fact. Open plate-racks sat beside attractively glazed wall cupboards, and dressers incorporated decorative fretwork. The kitchen became the most important room in the house and people were willing to spend the kind of money that just 15 years previously would have bought a house. It was the age of the custom-built kitchen and scores of entrepreneurial designers leapt on the bandwagon.

The 1980s saw further decline in the desire for a separate dining room as eating in the kitchen became more and more popular. Today a house with a kitchen too small to accommodate a table is often rejected by would-be buyers. The modern kitchen (*below*) is once more the heart of the home. There is likely to be a mix of textures: bricks and stone softened with distressed paintwork or marble set into wooden work surfaces and a large farmhouse table taking centre stage. Only low-key technology is visible, with appliances discreetly hidden behind integrated cupboard doors. Today's kitchen must be practical, but it also has to be 'eye-sweet'.
Gardiner's Homecare, Bristol/Smallbone of Devizes (2)

go gay with Fablon REGD.

SELF-ADHESIVE

FLECK *also Buff, Blue, Primrose, Red and Pink.*

KIMBERLEY *also on White ground.*

STARDOM *also Yellow, Red, Lilac, Black, Blue, Grey and Red on White.*

VINO *also on White ground.*

GINGHAM *also Green, Yellow, Blue.*

WOOD GRAIN *also Walnut and Maple.*

FABLON *transforms* your home—so easily, so economically. Give the kitchen table a new, gleaming surface; smarten that shelf; cover that door; decorate that tray. Everywhere in the house the beauty of FABLON will bring endless pleasure—and leisure. Self-adhesive FABLON is so simple to use—just cut it to shape (instructions on the "Easistrip" backing paper) and smooth it into position. Here is just a sample of Fablon's latest Spring collection of up-to-the-minute designs and colours. Never has there been such a galaxy! See and handle this beautiful material at your paint and wallpaper dealer, hardware or department store.

There are two widths and qualities:

Fablon   **Fablon TOP**

FABLON *is 18" wide, sells at 3/9 yd. It is ideal for decorating walls, doors, nursery furniture, drawers and shelves.*

FABLON TOP *is double-thick and 36" wide and sells at 10/6 yd. Its extra thickness makes it ideal for table and working surfaces.*

MOSAIC *also Red, Green and Grey.*

MILKY WAY *also Red, Yellow and Black.*

CARNIVAL

PLAIN *also White, Black and Yellow.*

Proud Products
49 PARK LANE

22

Note the use of the word 'gay' in this 1959 Fablon advertisement, meaning light-hearted and brightly coloured; this original meaning has since disappeared from our vocabulary, and would never be used in this context today.

At 3s 9d per yard, Fablon was a self-adhesive, wipe-clean plastic covering, and probably did more to revamp tired kitchens and dreary bedsits than any other decorating product. The company's advertising slogan 'Go Gay With Fablon' meant just that. It came in a wide range of designs from plains, flecks, stripes and checks to small geometric prints, which were popular for the period. Eye-catching colours predominated, including red, green, yellow and blue, as well as black.

'Fablon was my answer to everything,' recalls one housewife of the time. 'You see, women didn't do much decorating then - it was considered a man's job. But Fablon could be cut with scissors, the backing peeled off and stuck on whatever you fancied. For a few shillings I transformed my old-fashioned kitchen. The end result was a mishmash of colour and pattern, which at the time I thought was frightfully modern - the 1950s answer to the designer touch.'

Storey's Contact was another similar and well remembered product.

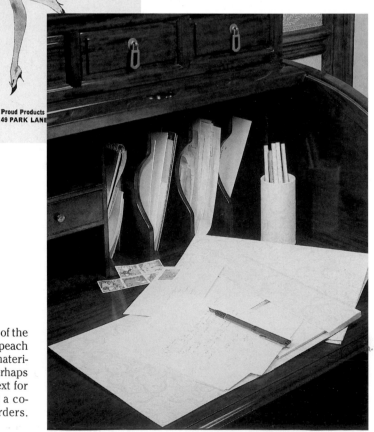

Now costing £1.50-£2.00 per metre, Fablon reflects the mood of the '90s. Colours are softer and more subtle - pink, coral, lilac, peach and ochre - while designs meet today's demand for natural materials like marble, wood, cork and granite. Fablon's use has perhaps shifted and women are more likely to use it in a craft context for making desk accessories, picture frames or for bringing a co-ordinated look to their homes with pretty stencilled borders.
Forbo-CP Ltd

Plastic laminate first made its appearance in British kitchens shortly after the Second World War, and has been the most popular kitchen worktop ever since. It is made from sheets of chemically soaked paper baked to form a hard surface, then bonded on to dense wood particle board. In the early days laminate was only available as a flat sheet; an edging piece had to be glued on, and joins were covered with metal or plastic strips, which were notorious for harbouring gunge! Formica was to become a household name and was largely responsible for revolutionising kitchens throughout the country. Indeed, such was the company's success that the name 'Formica' has become synonymous with all plastic laminates.

After centuries of scrubbing wooden work surfaces and living with dull enamelled or linoleum table-tops, here was a material that was germproof, heat resistant to 310°F, would not crack, chip or stain, and could be cleaned in a couple of minutes with a damp cloth. Above all, its colourful glossy surface perfectly suited the contemporary look of the 1950s.

In 1955 there were 40 designs to choose from, including Corinth Pink, Scarlet Red and Green Onyx, as well as wood-grain finishes such as Bleached Mahogany. Formica's use soon spread from the kitchen to transform dining tables, coffee tables, cocktail cabinets, desks, shelves and chests of drawers.

Colour photographs by courtesy of Ezee Kitchens Ltd. Also shown: De La Rue G.5 gas cooker and Kenwood mixer.

Clean at a wipe!

NO TROUBLE AT ALL to cope with cleaning up when your working tops are all 'FORMICA'. Swish a damp cloth over this hard non-porous surface and every trace of grease and dirt is gone. Scrubbing and polishing are things of the past wherever 'FORMICA' comes into your home. Isn't it time you enjoyed your share of the extra leisure and freedom 'FORMICA' can give you—every day of your life?

FORMICA LAMINATED PLASTIC
MADE BY **DE LA RUE**

Today's plastic laminates can be formed to make round-edge worktops - known as post-formed - or they can be successfully edged with other materials to provide a neat and hygienic surface. Suppliers can now pre-cut laminate in fairly complex shapes, minimising the number of joins, and coloured sealants create virtually invisible seams. There are high-gloss laminates, comparable with lacquer finishes, and dramatic designs based on the natural landscape that reflect oceans, storms and deserts.

But perhaps the wonder worktop of recent years is Du Pont's Corian, a solid surfacing material made by the fusion of natural mineral and acrylic. It can be sculptured into flowing curves and moulded into sinks, bowls and draining recesses for inconspicuous integration. Corian offers today's housewife a hard durable work surface that stays looking good with the minimum of effort.
Formica Ltd/MB

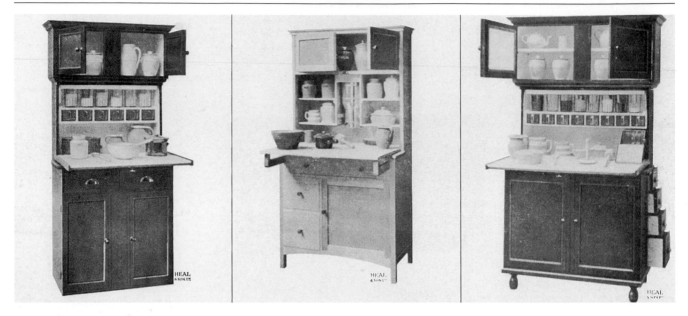

Probably the biggest single development in kitchen furniture, and the precursor to the fitted kitchens that followed, was the free-standing multi-purpose cabinet. First designed in the 1920s for the ever-shrinking kitchens of the time, they were the modern answer to bulky and unfashionable Victorian dressers.

Multi-purpose cabinets were compact pieces of furniture and were either left in their natural wood state or painted. Concealed behind the drop-down or pull-out enamelled flap was a series of shelves and compartments. Some designs incorporated innovative features such as flour dispensers, egg holders, storage jars, hooks, spice drawers and ventilation grilles for storing fresh food. Three sold by Heal's in the 1930s are seen here, and such cabinets remained enormously popular throughout the 1940s and '50s. *Heal's*

Some 50 years later, the crowning glory to the unfitted look of modern kitchens is the Victorian-style dresser! While original examples are much sought after, specialist companies produce some wonderful designs in a range of natural woods or painted finishes. This free-standing dresser can be made in the size and colour of your choice; the worktop and knobs are crafted in solid maple and it costs about £2,350. *McFadden cabinetmakers, Bath*

Serving hatches were a product of the 1920s and '30s, built into modern houses as a labour-saving feature. Because the supply of butlers, cooks and maids had dwindled to a trickle between the wars, the installation of a hatch was considered a modern convenience to the servantless housewife, or her meagre domestic help if she had any.

Together with the ubiquitous hostess trolley, serving hatches were regarded as great savers of time and effort, and even mini status symbols. Meals could be passed through the little double doors, which alleviated the chore of carrying heavy trays of hot food along corridors and halls. Similarly, dirty dishes were passed back through the hatch, then whisked into the sink by the housewife or maid. *W. W. Winter*

Serving hatches remained popular throughout the 1960s, then, with the arrival of the kitchen/diner, they rather faded from fashion. Many were bricked up or the wall knocked down and formed into an arch between the two rooms. Today serving hatches are either loved or hated. Mike Pegler of Fareham says, 'I find mine handy to ask friends if they want coffee or whatever. It's better than yelling, which no one hears anyway over the noise of music or the TV. I can just pop my head through the hatch and talk normally.' *MB*

GOODBYE MR THERM

The smiling face of Britain's gas industry personified - 'Mr Therm' - had been used in advertisements since the days of the Gas, Light & Coke Company in the 1930s, and is seen here (*below*) welcoming visitors to the Festival of Britain in 1951. However, by the beginning of the 1960s the public regarded gas as dirty, smelly, dangerous and old-fashioned, and in 1962 'Mr Therm' was sacked by advertising agents Colman, Prentis & Varley - but if gas was regarded as a dying industry, daring and radical action was called for.

The agency decided that instead of plugging gas appliances, which had hitherto been the case, they would promote gas itself, conveying a 'with it' image (the buzz words of the 1960s). Thus the slogan 'High Speed Gas' was born, which resulted in one of the most successful advertising campaigns ever - sales rose by 11 per cent in the first year.

Today, more than 30 years later, gas sales continue to grow. Conversion from coal gas to natural gas took place in the early 1970s, and it remains enormously popular for cooking and central heating.

Right This advertisement for the paradoxically named Electrolux gas refrigerator of the 1940s shows a bulky, cumbersome-looking appliance, despite its many attractive features. *Electrolux*

CURTAIN UP ON Mr. THERM
at the Festival

While Britain is at home to the world, Mr. Therm — Britain's gas industry personified — is lending a helping hand everywhere . . . just as usual. Gas, for example, is taking care of the heating and cooking in the fine new Royal Festival Hall, and Mr. Therm is very busy in the kitchens serving the South Bank exhibition restaurants. Gas, too, has had an important part in the making of many of the exhibits. All over Britain, gas makes things easier in the home, and provides the plentiful hot water essential for healthy conditions where food is prepared and handled. And the use of gas and its companion fuel, coke, helps to get rid of fog, for both are smokeless. Besides gas and coke, gas-making produces many valuable synthetic products from coal—drugs, dyes, plastics, fertilisers and many more, of the greatest use to all of us.

So please accept a welcome from Mr. Therm. You'll find that he's helping you, in all sorts of unexpected ways, all over Britain . . . .

GAS AT YOUR SERVICE

ISSUED BY THE GAS COUNCIL

The *New* ELECTROLUX

Air-Cooled
GAS
Refrigerator

MODEL LJP

MODEL L J P

● Specification ●

STORAGE CAPACITY : $5\frac{1}{2}$ cubic feet.

SHELF AREA : 9.8 square feet.

ICE MAKING : Approx. 3 lbs. of ice per freezing. 3 trays (one rubber) with partitions. Each tray 16 cubes.

INTERNAL LINING : Porcelain enamel on steel.

EXTERNAL DIMENSIONS :
  Height (with feet) - 4 ft. $9\frac{1}{8}$ ins.
  Width - - - 2 ft. $3\frac{5}{8}$ ins.
  Depth (excluding door furniture) - - 2 ft. $3\frac{3}{4}$ ins.

EXTERNAL FINISH : White washable cellulose enamelled steel.

BRITISH MADE.

Features : Automatic temperature regulation with ten-point control incorporating "Defrost" and "Quick-Freezing" settings. Enclosed ice-making compartment. Porcelain-enamelled radiator cover. Quick release ice trays. Utility basket (for eggs and vegetables). Large Vitaliser (for crisping salads, etc.). Set of three glass dishes. Five steel shelves (two adjustable and sliding). Rounded corners inside, and broom-high legs. Chromium-plated door furniture with snap action door-lock. Simplified lighting device. Modern design and beautiful finish. No moving parts. Silent operation. No radio interference.

Cash Price
£52'10.

THE FLAME THAT FREEZES

ELECTROLUX—THE GAS REFRIGERATOR

Bringing the joys of refrigeration to every home !

New "Family" Frigidaire for only £89.19.0

No other refrigerator gives you so much for so little money. Keeps a whole week's shopping Frigidaire-fresh !

Has your family had to manage without a refrigerator ? You needn't any longer—for here's the new, low-price "Family" Frigidaire ! Now you, too, can protect family health . . . serve tastier meals . . . turn entertaining into fun. You can keep food fresh in any weather, save housekeeping money by avoiding waste, enjoy more leisure. When food keeps till it's needed, once-a-week shopping is ample !

This fine table-top Frigidaire is easy on kitchen space, generous in storage room. Though only 2 ft. square by 3 ft. high, it gives more than 4 cu. ft. of inside storage space—enough for all the family needs !

But the best way to learn about the "Family" Frigidaire is to see it for yourself at Frigidaire Dealers, Electricity Board Service Centres and all large stores.

Holds enough food for all the family

Top-to-bottom refrigeration—so *no* waste space. All perishable food is kept fresh, wholesome and safe from germs and deterioration. And more food *inside* your refrigerator means that you have more free kitchen and larder space *outside* !

Represents the woman's point of view !

In a country-wide survey by the *Electrical Association for Women*, housewives listed these features as specially desirable in a refrigerator : work-table top, quiet running, frozen food storage space, compact design.

See how the "Family" Frigidaire scores on these points !

White acid-resistant porcelain table-top with splash back. So durable it won't scratch, chip or stain even when you slice bread or cut meat on it. *Extra quiet "Meter-Miser" power unit*—radio and TV suppressed—uses less current than an ordinary light bulb and is backed by a 5-Year Warranty.
Big Super Freezer stores 12 lb. of frozen foods or ice cream.
Frigidaire design produces a marvel of compactness.

Other special features include :—

Quick-Release Ice Tray ; Adjustable Cold Control ; easily cleaned interior—acid-resistant porcelain lining, rounded corners, removable shelves ; all-steel cabinet with 1-Year Warranty ; smooth exterior — wipes clean instantly.

Early refrigerators were bulky with a monstrous cooling motor sited on top of the cabinet. Gradually designs became neater and the curvaceous shape we associate with the 1950s gave way to the more angular, slimline models we know today. The advert for the 'Family' Frigidaire (*left*) dates from the summer of 1953, while the photograph (*above*) shows a range of fridges on display in an electricity showroom in the 1950s, including Coldrator and Kelvinator models.

In 1959 fridges appeared on the market incorporating small freezer compartments, although these were barely big enough for an ice-cube tray and a block of ice-cream.

For households without a fridge (the majority of the population), keeping perishables for any length of time was impossible. Housewives living in towns were forced to shop almost daily, whereas country folk, without easy access to shops, implemented alternative methods of preservation. Fruit and vegetables, once harvested, were laid on straw in a shed or garage, while potatoes were put into a trench in the ground and covered with soil and straw to provide frost-free storage.

Tom Hally recalls, 'My father used to check our potato store once a month. He usually had terriers standing by in case rats had got in. Any rotten potatoes were fed to the pigs and the remainder covered over again.'

Few, if any, modern kitchens are without a fridge. Here (*right*) the fashion for concealing technology is echoed in the integrated fridge with its door matching the kitchen furniture.

Although the first frozen foods became available in the late 1930s, the average housewife knew little about what was on the market and how it should be stored or cooked. The introduction of frozen food and home freezers was a major step forward in food storage, eliminating the problems of seasonality and the necessity for daily shopping. Home freezers were on sale in Britain as early as 1956, but even by 1972 only 5.8 per cent of households had one; in 1994 the figure was 34 per cent.

Sales of individual fridges and freezers declined with the arrival of the all-in-one fridge-freezer. This American fridge-freezer of 1948 (*above right*) was revolutionary at the time - as usual the Americans were ahead of the game when it came to domestic appliances. It was over 20 years before fridge-freezers appeared on the domestic scene in Britain, as exemplified by this Electrolux example from 1970 (*above*). In 1994, 56 per cent of households owned this popular dual appliance.

Then in the mid-1970s a mini boom took place, and chest freezers were the thing to be seen in upwardly mobile kitchens. Housewives flocked to buy quarters of beef, sides of pork and whole lambs. The idea was that it saved money to buy in bulk, but was that the case in reality? Not according to one housewife of the time.

'If we couldn't sleep we'd often get up for a snack - something like cheese and biscuits or a bowl of cereal - but after we filled our new freezer with meat, we'd rustle up a fillet steak instead. We may have eaten better but we certainly didn't save money!'

Today, if we so desire, we can enjoy raspberries at Christmas and plum pudding in July thanks to the freezer revolution. In times of glut we can buy cheaply knowing that we can store produce for months at a time without fear of deterioration. Many modern fridge-freezers are frost-free, meaning that with the dry blown air system there is no need ever to defrost fridge or freezer. This 1996 Electrolux model (*right*) is aimed at a new growth market - the smaller household. Interestingly, statistics show that over half the population is made up of one- or two-person households. *Good Housekeeping/Electrolux (2)*

3. COOKING

Above left In 1939 any steps forward in domestic appliance manufacture were halted when production switched to munitions. In 1945, however, things started to return to normal and Belling produced its famous VEE cooker, remembered by thousands of prefab dwellers. This 1947 model, similar to the VEE, boasts a thermostat; these were first fitted to electric ovens in 1938 and gas ovens in 1923.

Many cookers with the old 'low', 'medium' and 'high' controls were in use in post-war years, but housewives devised their own method of testing oven temperatures. A favourite was the greaseproof paper test. If the paper turned pale fawn in 10 minutes, the temperature was about 350°F or regulo 4 and was suitable for sponges and medium-sized cakes. If the paper turned golden brown in 5 minutes, the temperature had reached 400°F or regulo 6, and was ready to cook scones and pastry. If the paper turned rich brown in 5 minutes, it was suitable for Yorkshire pudding, having reached 450°F or regulo 8. *Belling Appliances Ltd*

Above right The majority of cookers were constructed from iron with a cream or grey vitreous enamelled finish, although this 1949 GEC cooker was also available in green and cream. The development of pressed sheet steel enabled cookers to be squared off at floor level rather than standing on legs. This allowed space for a storage drawer and warming compartment.

An oblong hotplate was usually incorporated into the hob under which the grill was situated. *South Western Electricity Historical Society*

One housewife remembers buying a second-hand gas cooker like this one for £2 in 1951. 'We called it Alfred because it burned everything, including the linoleum underneath,' she says. 'The legs became red hot, so we eventually stood it on a metal sheet, otherwise it would have probably gone through the floor!

'The cooker was mottled black and white cast iron with a million parts and was a brute to clean. All those heavy and cumbersome burners and pipes. I'd soak them in a bucket of boiling water and soda, then scrub until my hands were raw. Some parts I never could get clean, so I just threw them away!

'Ten years later we finally got rid of Alfred. I felt so guilty, it was like discarding a friend. I can still see him being driven away in the back of an open truck. All the children were waving goodbye.'

Fan-assisted ovens were introduced in the 1980s, which reduced the need for pre-heating and offered faster, more even cooking at lower temperatures. Today's housewife can even have the choice of a combination cooker with gas hob and electric oven.

Recent years have seen the introduction of touch-control panels instead of raised knobs, halogen hobs (which glow red giving virtually instant heat) and deep-fat fryers, barbecue grills and griddles incorporated into hobs.

Although split-level cookers remain as popular as ever, there is a growing trend towards range-style models to complement period kitchens. In line with other major manufacturers, this Belling Farmhouse was launched in 1995 - it looks uncannily like their 1960 Super Seventy (*below right*), but it is a modern appliance with all the style, capacity and appeal of a traditional range. *Belling Appliances Ltd*

IN GAS COOKERS

Colour is the coming thing

(AND LOOK WHAT COMES WITH IT)

WHY NOT let's have cookers in gay, fresh colours to harmonize with modern kitchens? Above, the De La Rue "Warwick" Gas Cooker in cheerful green and cream. Another model is in grey, white and burgundy. AND *WHAT* A COOKER! The oven, 17″ wide, 18″ high and 13″ deep, will house the largest turkey—and all its trimmings. The grill is at eye level and toasts four large slices at a time—evenly. A four-hour timer to take the guesswork out of cooking. Safety taps, of course, and *five* full size boiling burners to handle the most ambitious meal.

Cleaning? Easier than ever. The pan rests go into the washing up bowl and a whisk with a damp cloth keeps the hotplate immaculate.

WILL IT FIT YOUR KITCHEN? The "Warwick" is 30″ x 23½″. We will send you an exact template so that you can make sure. Also a fully illustrated leaflet—just send us your name and address. Better still, see the "Warwick" at your nearest Gas Showroom. For a few shillings a week this, the most luxurious domestic gas cooker in Britain can be yours.

DE LA RUE *Warwick* GAS COOKER

DE LA RUE GAS COOKERS THOMAS DE LA RUE & CO. LTD. (GAS DIVISION) DEPT. G.H. 84/86 REGENT STREET, LONDON, W.1

In the 1950s, when hire purchase was more readily available and a housewife's status was measured by her prowess as a cook, an up-to-the-minute gas or electric cooker became the be all and end all, as this advert from 1954 testifies.

MANY NEW FEATURES...

Autotimers (*bottom left*) made their debut fitted to cookers around the late 1950s. Food could now be placed in the oven and programmed to switch on and off at pre-set times. However, the cook had to understand the 24-hour clock; although quite simple given a little common sense, to many housewives at the time it was a newfangled idea. A friend recalls waking up in the small hours of Christmas morning to the delicious aroma of roast turkey all cooked and ready to eat!

In the early days of autotimers, inaccurate setting was one of the biggest reasons for engineers and fitters to be called out in response to 'My oven won't come on'. Invariably someone in the household had fiddled with the timer; once the clock was set for automatic start, the oven would not come on manually.

Competing designers offered all manner of modern features, some more gimmicky than others. As early as 1945 Belling produced a see-through inner glass door, which alleviated the problem of blasts of cold air causing cakes to sink when the outer door was opened. In 1960 Creda introduced their Rosta-Spit (*below*), which rotated inside the oven.

In 1963 Tricity launched its Melodie (*opposite page*), the first - and only - cooker with a built-in transistor radio, literally in tune with the vibrant '60s! It is also interesting to note that a stow-away fan heater was available to warm kitchens before the days when central heating became the norm. Ceramic hobs appeared on the market in 1966, and in the 1970s came self-clean ovens.

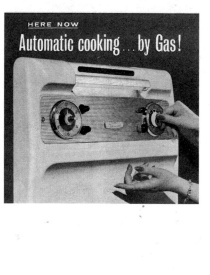

HERE NOW
Automatic cooking... by Gas!

make the most exciting home cooking news of the century...

...*a revolutionary new electric cooker with the exclusive*

CREDA ROSTA-SPIT
and sensational CREDA GRIDDLE!

Every woman knows that *even* heat is essential to all good cooking. And since only an oven can give all-round *even* heat, Creda designed this ingenious Rosta-Spit to rotate inside the wonderful oven of the new MERCURY SUPER FOUR. So now you have the best of *both* worlds ... rotary spit and oven-cooking combined.

The Creda Griddle is a die-cast aluminium plate that sits neatly over the front two Creda quick-discs on the hob and gives you *griddle*-cooked steaks, chops, bacon-and-eggs ... *delicious!* Griddle baking too ... Drop Scones, Welsh Cakes, Pikelets and a host of others.

Here then are all the succulent joys of Rotisserie cooking in your own oven ... and delightful griddle cooking too. This and more *in the Creda Mercury Super Four*, look ...

● **SUPER FAST.** All four quick-discs are very fast, one is specially boosted for fastest boiling ever; each is separately controlled from a gentle simmer to a steady boil.

● **EASIEST TO CLEAN.** Four quick-discs, exclusive to Creda, are sealed to the hob for easiest wipe-over cleaning ever.

● **NEW EASY WORKING HEIGHT.** Sensible new hob height of 33 inches (3 inch plinth available at small extra cost for those with 36 inch high kitchen units).

● **LESS STOOPING.** Oven raised to more convenient height.

● **SEALED INNER GLASS DOOR** and automatic oven interior light, you see "what's cooking" *without* loss of heat.

● **LARGE WARMING DRAWER** separately heated, also provides storage for grill pan and griddle.

● **LARGE FULLY AUTOMATIC OVEN** designed for perfection in timer-controlled cooking. Takes 28 lb. turkey. Oven, Rosta-Spit, Warming Drawer all controlled by automatic timer.

● **CLOCK FACE TIMER,** simple-to-set (for remote control cooking). Five-hour ringer.

● **HIGH SPLASH PLATE** and luxurious control panel (out of children's reach).

● **CREDA SEALATCH,** finger-light, click close.

● **LARGE EVEN-HEATING GRILL** Six slices of toast at a time.

In white or cream enamel.

NO EXTRAS

Other Creda cookers available from £27.10.0.

55 GNS.

CREDA ROSTA-SPIT IN THE BEST PLACE

See the NEW Creda Mercury Super Four NOW! at your local Electrical Showroom

Creda Ltd

British food has always been the butt of jokes. A slogan seen recently on an American tee-shirt read 'Hell is where the chef is British', and I recall a line from a Tony Hancock show to the effect of 'I thought my mother was a bad cook but at least her gravy moved about'.

In spite of early television cookery presenters such as Marguerite Patten and Fanny Craddock, few housewives seemed to rise above meat and two veg. When I was growing up in the 1950s, food - even at the time - seemed to be incredibly boring. Of course there wasn't the choice of ingredients, nor was there the inclination for creative cooking. Mushrooms were considered an exotic extravagance, and avocado pears were the stuff of science fiction.

Our meals were the plain, no frills type that were typical of the period. I can still remember what we ate each day of the week - it hardly changed. There was roast meat on Sundays and rissoles or cottage pie, made with the left-overs, on Monday. In the middle of the week we had stew, with fish on Fridays. Everything was accompanied by potatoes in various guises and a boiled vegetable - mother's idea of cordon bleu was a white sauce on cauliflower! There was always desert, something like fruit crumble, apple pie, rice pudding, bananas and custard or steamed syrup pudding.

On Saturdays we had what was commonly referred to as High Tea, a tradition that developed around the turn of the century as a working man's early supper. It was usually cold meat, smoked haddock or cheese on toast, a cake and maybe fruit jelly or blancmange. My father hated meals like that - he wondered where his meat and two veg were - but mother retaliated by saying that she'd spent enough time in the kitchen during the week.

In the early 1960s I can remember being taken to an Indian restaurant, probably one of the first outside London. I couldn't have been more excited by this change in convention and wonderful alien-tasting food than if I'd flown to Bombay itself. Cooking was becoming more extrovert and gaining an international flavour. The days of the severely traditional British meal were in decline. Fuelled by the influx of foreign immigrants, gradually more unusual produce started to appear in shops and the newly designed supermarkets. Also, Mr & Mrs Jones had travelled widely enough to be on intimate terms with garlic, fresh herbs, aubergines, artichokes and olive oil, although at the time the only olive oil available was sold in little bottles for medicinal purposes by chemists.

In the 1970s a positive paranoia about food set in. Diets and health issues became big business, and the debate about what is good for you and what is not still continues. In 1945 there were

Family cooking, 1950s-1990s. *Good Housekeeping/Belling Appliances Ltd*

The man who loves Tuesdays

FRED used to hate Tuesdays. "Stewsday", he'd mutter dolefully, walking up the path. Kate, clever little woman, noticed. Now Fred gets home earlier on Tuesdays. This is what she did.

Here's the easy recipe—HIGH HAT STEW

1 *lb. lean beef*
2 *level teasps. Bovril*
2 *carrots*
1 *onion*
6 *ozs. suet crust*
2 *tablesps. dripping*
Salt and pepper

Roll meat in flour and lightly fry in dripping with sliced onion. Put in a saucepan or casserole with tight-fitting lid. Add diced carrots, Bovril and seasoning. Cover with cold water, boil up and simmer 1½ hours. Roll crust to size of pan, place on top of meat and cook gently with lid on for 30-40 minutes.

All cooked dishes are all the better for Bovril

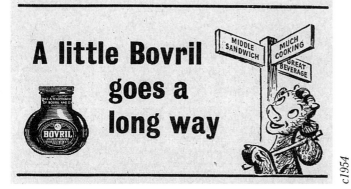

A little Bovril goes a long way

c1954

"I look forward to Steak & Kidney Pudding every Saturday..."

It's best made with

ATORA

READY-SHREDDED BEEF SUET

Atora makes the most deliciou puddings and dumplings ever Turn your hand to Jam Rol Poly or Spotted Dick for Sunda 'afters'—they are good to ea and good for the family.

★ *Send P.C. for ATORA Recipe Boo to Hugon & Co., Manchester II.*

c1952

100,000 registered vegetarians; in 1994 the figure was 2.5 million. Over the last 25 years, vegetarian food has become very sophisticated and in many cases it is impossible to realise that you are not eating meat. Even if families are not strict vegetarians, many housewives cook some meatless meals each week.

In the 1980s, fuelled by scares over red meat and cholesterol, came a new 'foodie' revolution - nouvelle cuisine. However, the idea of minute portions of food all laid out geometrically and garnished with radish roses and carrot curls was short-lived. Come the 1990s, everyone was into sun-dried tomatoes and couscous!

In our times of gastronomic plenty, it is hard to define a typical family meal. In a single week there could be anything on the menu from Lancashire hot-pot to a herb-enhanced designer salad. And you're just as likely to see parents eating Salmon Hollandaise (courtesy of M&S) while the kids tuck into chicken nuggets and fries (courtesy of Birds Eye)!

Christmas preparations used to start in our house in October. I remember mother 'plumping up' dried fruit in big basins of water before making her Christmas cake. Then there was the pungent aroma of baking, and weeks later the laborious job of marzipanning and icing, often done late into the night. Some time in November she made Christmas puddings, cooked in little china bowls that were completely wrapped in squares of white cloth tied on the top turban-style; usually old pillow-cases were commandeered for the job.

Currants, raisins and sultanas were rationed during the war. Monica Bourke recalls how her mother bought little bits each week, starting months before Christmas, so that she could make cakes and puddings. Jean Hadden remembers that her family's rations wouldn't stretch to buying icing sugar, so her mother stuck a circle of white cardboard on the cake instead!

In 1962, when this Christmas 'past' was photographed, turkey was a treat and only afforded for special occasions. Today it costs marginally more per pound than Brussels sprouts. Today's family Christmas is usually a more relaxed affair. If she so desires, today's housewife can choose an almost instant frozen and/or ready prepared Christmas dinner. *Allan Mott/Chris Hughes*

Past and Present colour
Home Sweet Home

Bright outlook

This housewife might be smiling as she cooks a family meal in her bright modern kitchen, but most women found the reality quite different. For this was 1948, the age of austerity. The average housewife worked in dull, spartan and ill-planned kitchens, and feeding her family was a time-consuming and difficult task. Rations were even lower than they had been during the war.

'You'd have to queue for hours just to buy a piece of imported bacon, which was pure fat,' recalls Brenda Dix. 'We used to stuff and fry it.'

Monica Bourke also remembers sides of fatty bacon hanging in her local grocer's shop. 'There was no cold storage then,' she explains, 'and in hot weather the bacon was crawling with maggots, but housewives still bought it.'

In an effort to appease British housewives, whale meat was introduced by the Government. Then came snoek, a South African fish, but even at 1 shilling per tin, it remained hugely unpopular. 'You didn't really know what you were eating. It could have been baboon for all we knew,' says another housewife of the time.

There was also a fuel shortage, and many housewives recall taking their prepared Sunday lunch to the local baker's shop for cooking in his large ovens. Housewifery books and magazines did their best to encourage housewives to plan for a bright future. There was a new awareness in kitchen planning making for a more rational arrangement of furniture and fittings.

'Functional' became the buzz word of the late 1940s. Those who could afford to modernise their kitchens took advantage of the modular unit furniture that was appearing on the market, and families were realising the benefit of eating occasional meals in the kitchen. If space allowed, a small dining bay was separated from the work area by a divider. In this photograph open shelves are constructed above a peninsula cupboard fixture. The arrangement conceals clutter when the family is eating, maximises light and space and provides useful storage facilities.

Bright colours and easy-clean surfaces epitomised the modern 1940s kitchen. Cream was enormously popular and was often combined with touches of red, blue, green or yellow.

Today's housewife has none of the struggle of her counterpart of 50 years ago, although her life is as busy as ever. Technological advancement and the huge variety of food available in specialist shops and supermarkets have enabled her to reduce substantially the amount of time she spends preparing and cooking food. Convenience has become an accepted watchword in the kitchen, allowing women more choice in the way they allocate their time. This attractive kitchen boasts all the latest appliances enabling its owner to knock off the family wash in hours rather than days. She is no longer forced to shop on a daily basis, as she can preserve food for months in her freezer. Bar stools and a split-level divider provide a handy spot for family meals and, in line with informal modern eating, a wall-mounted television ensures that no-one misses their favourite programme! *Good Housekeeping/ Will Adams courtesy of Jane Piercy-Hughes*

Looking one's best

In 1948, even if it could be afforded, reliable daily help was impossible to find. Girls who had been maids before the war were earning good money in shops, offices and factories. The demands on the housewife were therefore never-ending, even though equipment and appliances, unknown to her mother, were on the market.

The reality was that few had them. The modern woman found herself playing many roles - wife, mother, housekeeper, cook, washerwoman, housemaid - and each year the DIY movement brought a new field of activity into a woman's life. Thus journalists were full of advice as to how housewives could look their best while coping with hectic domestic schedules.

The main criterion was to set aside a little time each day for herself. The over-40s were encouraged to take a midday rest 'to iron out the stiffness and strain of perpetual effort'! And 10 minutes in the middle of the day spent with her feet raised right off the ground was said to add years to her life.

Housewives were encouraged to look their best for husbands and family. Apparently a shiny nose, even at breakfast, was not a welcome sight! Neat hair, a clean frock or overall, tidy shoes and a lightly creamed and powdered face were early-morning musts. And however busy her day had been, she should change her frock and renew her make-up before the family returned in the evening. . .

Although many women still play a traditional role in caring for their partner and family, they have more time to spend on themselves. Few housewives today would even bother to look in the mirror pending the arrival of the breadwinner, far less change into something smart. Convenience foods, the two-car family, efficient domestic appliances, better diet, a wealth of cosmetic products, less strenuous housework and good inexpensive clothing have all played their part in offering housewives a more mentally fulfilling lifestyle. *Good Housekeeping/MB*

There is only one word that describes this kitchen and the two young housewives of 1960 - trendy! They are wearing the latest thing in early-morning fashion known as a 'breakfast set'. Both the shirtwaister and tunic and the trousers are made from drip-dry and non-iron 'Super Tremendo' fabric, and were designed to ensure breakfast-cooking wives looked pretty! The kitchen is one of many that could be seen at the time at that top-of-the-range department store - Harrods. Today it would probably make the management blush with embarrassment! *Good Housekeeping*

State of the art

Like it or loathe it, this 1952 English Rose kitchen was state-of-the-art at the time. It featured colour-co-ordinated and integrated units and appliances including fridge, cooker, pull-out trolley and even air-conditioning. As the advertisement states, it was aimed primarily at the export market. Even if such luxury could be afforded, there was a long waiting list. Britain was desperate for money and the need for export had to be met.

This up-to-the-minute kitchen is hand-ragged and marbled. The latest appliances are certainly there, but they are not flaunted; the overall atmosphere is one of ease and understatement. *Author's collection/MB*

The perfect hostess

In the 1950s the housewife-hostess reigned supreme; dinner and cocktail parties were the high point of socialising. With more food becoming available, housewives were expected to dish up interesting and attractive meals usually aimed at impressing her friends, her husband and his boss. Her highest accolade was when she was praised for her efforts and talked about for her good taste.

It was the era when business entertaining was done at home. Career success was won or lost on the housewife's prowess as a cook-hostess. It was also important that she looked the part - seen and not heard! Women's magazines of the time featured a wealth of patterns for hostess outfits that boasted such details as décolleté necklines and waists swathed in cummerbunds.

As life moved into the fast lane for women in the 1960s, so the amount of entertaining done at home declined. Good-quality ready-prepared food aided and abetted the road to freedom. Today's husband wouldn't dare phone up 10 minutes before arriving home to say he's bringing his boss for dinner - would he? His wife's reply would probably be something like, 'Tough luck, darling, it's my yoga class tonight!'

One modern corporate wife reports that her husband's business entertaining is largely conducted at restaurants. On the odd occasion that she is called upon to provide a special meal at home, she is likely to buy from the local department store food hall. *Author's collection*

Hot water on tap

No wonder this 1948 housewife is smiling - no more struggling with buckets of water or stoking coke boilers! She has installed the latest instantaneous gas water heater in her kitchen. Gradually these were seen in more and more homes, with 'Ascot' being a well remembered gas model, and 'Sadia' the electric equivalent.

This Ideal solid fuel boiler was another popular method of heating water. Note that it has the power to heat one radiator *or* a towel rail!

Thousands of sink water heaters are still in operation, especially in rented flats and bedsits. However, the majority of modern households enjoy a piped hot water system, either by means of a tank and immersion heater or a boiler. The latter have become smaller yet more powerful, not only providing hot water but also heating a dozen or so radiators. Clocks are pre-set to come on and off automatically at the most convenient times to suit the household's lifestyle. Some boilers, like this gas-fired model, are so inconspicuous that they fit into a kitchen cupboard behind an integrated door. *Good Housekeeping/author's collection/MB*

Chill factors

In 1948 a glass of ice-cold milk was a luxury, and freeze was something that happened in winter! Only a lucky few owned a refrigerator, although electric, gas and oil powered models were available; in 1946 just 2.2 per cent of households owned an electric fridge.

Advertisements (this one is dated about 1952) stressed low running costs - only a few pennies a week - and the advantage of not having to shop daily. Most housewives relied on a larder, which was situated on the north or east side of the kitchen and often had stone floor and shelves. Small free-standing meat and pie safes, with wire mesh doors, were also popular.

Food storage was difficult without a fridge. Meat and fish had to be purchased almost daily, and that doyenne of household management, Mrs Beeton, advised housewives to do their shopping early to ensure both quality and choice. Joan Lynes recalls life without a fridge: 'To keep milk fresh for as long as possible, it was boiled immediately after delivery then placed by an open window to cool. During the war we had a Morrison shelter in our living room. The metal top was so cold that I'd set jellies on it!'

Although some fridges had the benefit of automatic de-frosting, usually this was a weekly chore for the housewife.

Today's refrigerators are smaller and neater and come in a variety of options - built-in, built-under, eye-level, pull-out, decor-panel and integrated - as well as frost-free models that require no de-frosting.

Old fridges are responsible for emitting harmful CFCs (chlorofluorocarbons) that damage the ozone layer, ozone-destroying chemicals being found in insulating foam and coolants. Most new fridges achieve a 50 per cent reduction in CFCs and recent regulations mean that refrigeration appliances are graded for energy consumption between A (most efficient) and G (least efficient).
Good Housekeeping/author's collection/MB

Merry Christmas!

For most women in the post-war decades, cooking the Christmas dinner meant 48 hours hard labour! The flustered housewife had been up since dawn, gutting, plucking, trussing, stuffing, basting, peeling and slicing, her apron splattered with turkey fat and her face the colour of a tropical sunset. Then came the last-minute juggling act of carving and serving the bird, which often resulted in congealed gravy, soggy sprouts and frayed tempers. But there's little chance of our festive martyr relaxing and enjoying the fruits of her labour - she is dashing back and forth with cranberry jelly, bread sauce, vegetable tureens and bottle openers, and checking that the saucepan, in which the pudding has been steaming since dawn, hasn't boiled dry.

And after the festivities are over, the turkey meat seems to last for ever. It is sandwiched, smorgasborded, curried, fricasseed, hotpotted and pilaffed until such time as the poor housewife daren't mention the word 'turkey' without fear of a domestic rebellion!

Today turkeys cost marginally more per pound than Brussels sprouts, while rising numbers of people are boycotting the seasonal bird and opting instead for beef, duck, goose or even a vegetarian 'roast'. Many celebrate at restaurants or on holiday abroad.

Today's family Christmas is potentially a more relaxed affair; indeed, if she so desires, the modern housewife can choose an almost instant Christmas dinner. Ready-stuffed turkey breast, or legs only, are widely available, cutting cooking time by more than half and putting paid to the post-Christmas turkey recycling. Turkey garnish kits, comprising stuffing balls, bacon rolls, mini sausages, turkey gravy and bread sauce take the slog out of preparation. Then there are frozen roast potatoes, 101 varieties of vegetable, ready-made brandy butter, mince pies, Christmas cakes and puds - everything from basic to luxury. And instead of steaming puddings for hours they can be cooked to perfection in a microwave within minutes.

Some may argue that it's not the same. Where is the excitement and atmosphere in a 'bought' Christmas? And therein perhaps lies the answer to all those people you hear nowadays saying 'It doesn't feel like Christmas'. *Good Housekeeping/courtesy of Chris Hughes*

Mixing it

Food mixers did not generally become available in the UK until after the Second World War. The famous Kenwood Chef was the brainchild of Kenneth Wood who, in 1947, founded Kenwood Manufacturing Ltd, based in Surrey. His aim was to design and sell products that would start out as luxuries and develop into necessities. His first product was a toaster, followed by a twin-beater mixer, but with increasing competition from America he needed something new. He returned to the drawing-board, and the Kenwood Electric Chef was launched at the 1950 Ideal Home Exhibition. It cost £19 10s 10d.

Advertisements of the period suggested that by using modern appliances, housewives could look glamorous despite the domestic demands made on them. In this example the woman is prettily dressed and she wears make-up and ear-rings. All she has to do is whisk off her frilly apron when her husband returns from work and greet him with a home-made cake she has rustled up in next to no time thanks to her new food mixer!

From one basic model has grown an entire range of machines, each with different attributes to meet changing tastes. Only the fashion and technology have changed in these two photographs. Today men as well as women use Kenwood's range of mixers, but as this picture illustrates, the company's philosophy that Kenwoods are handed down from generation to generation and from parents to children still holds good today. *Rejectamenta/ Kenwood Ltd*

New room, new man!

Bathrooms were spartan places in the 1940s, and until fairly recently were the most neglected room in the house - chilly, utilitarian and draughty. Decoration tended to be clinical, ugly exposed pipes banged and clanked and lucky indeed was the occupant who didn't fall victim to slippery wet lino. Cork-topped stools were a common feature - bidets were just as rare!

The bathroom is the last room to join our households. As recently as the 1970s, statistics show that one in ten English families did not have their own bathroom. Most suites were white, although green, primrose and pink were available. During the 1960s and '70s other pastel shades were introduced, with avocado proving particularly popular; white became distinctly undesirable. In the 1980s dark colours, such as navy blue and burgundy, were all the rage, and avocado was out! According to bathroom specialists, what everyone wants today is white - such are the vagaries of fashion.

The following words, written in the 1940s, epitomise what was expected of women at the time: 'It is of the first importance that a mother should devote herself to her home and her children as a full time job.' She took full responsibility and care for the children while her husband was expected to provide a background of economic security by going out to work. Prior to the Second World War, fathers hardly knew they had children until they were 9 or 10 years old!

Bathrooms today boast wall-to-wall carpeting, central heating, concealed plumbing, a never-ending supply of hot water and suites in a wide range of colours.

Although bidets have become normal bathroom equipment, they were slow to catch on in the UK. In the 1930s there was public outcry when the Ritz Hotel in New York installed them in its bathrooms; against mounting pressure they were finally removed, for bidets were French, were they not, and therefore naughty!

Historically men have been cushioned against the harsh realities of domestic life. Now, with so many married women working, men are expected to share household responsibilities. Indeed, in today's economic climate it is often the wife who is the breadwinner, with her partner playing a major role in caring for the children. 'New Man' was a product of the 1980s, not created by engineers but moulded by 'Superwoman'. She was a new breed and she wasn't prepared to wait on her family hand and foot. If there was one thing 'New Woman' was not prepared to tolerate, it was 'Old Man' - he belonged to the history books! *Good Housekeeping/MB*

Right In the late 1940s and well into the '50s, some households were still struggling with primitive cooking methods. Pat Hally recalls her mother cooking in iron kettles and pots that hung from hooks and ratchets over an open fire. In some homes there was an oven in the side of the chimney where bread was baked.

Large numbers of households were also still cooking by coal-fired range, although gas gradually replaced solid fuel. In 1946 only 16.6 per cent of households in England and Wales cooked by electricity.

As more and more families installed modern cooking facilities, so big open fireplaces like this one were boarded up and forgotten.

Are we guilty today of buying a lifestyle? We want a sophisticated version of the 1940s working kitchen - the image of country life but with none of the drudgery, as exemplified by this 'posed' modern advertisement for Aga (*below right*) with its pre-war ambience. One devotee remembers being evacuated during the war to a Cornish farmhouse that had an Aga.

'There was something very comforting about riddling the embers, and in winter, when the rest of the house was freezing, we'd get dressed for school in the kitchen. Our Aga was used for all sorts of things including drying clothes and coaxing chickens and piglets back from the brink of death. Once a cat had her kittens on top of it.'

Tom Hally recalls life in rural Ireland in the 1940s, '50s and '60s. 'Country dwellers needed a big cooker to cope with all the people constantly in and out of the kitchen. The Aga, with its hot and warm ovens, spacious hotplates and rail for drying towels, was considered a practical workhorse and rare was the farm or country house that didn't have one.

'Ours was the heart of the home. It stood in a chimney recess and my father would squeeze his chair into the space at the side - the warmest spot in the house. There was an integral water chamber that had to be filled daily from the well, but it meant we enjoyed constant hot water.'

The current 'lifestyle' kitchen (*left*) harks back to the rustic 'ideal' but with dishwasher, freezer and washing machine camouflaged behind panels of designer-distressed paintwork or chunks of stripped pine. Pulley-operated clothes dryers are now hung with dried flowers and baskets where once there would have been wet woollies and farmers' socks. Only low-key appliances are allowed to be seen and, yes, in that redundant chimney breast an Aga will do very nicely, thank you! The ultimate statement that the owner is rejecting the brash world and all the shiny plastic and modern technology that goes with it.

The Aga has become something of a cult and is just as likely to be seen in an elegant Georgian townhouse as humble country cottages and working farms. Its basic principles of design and operation have changed little in the last 50 years, which could explain why it is regarded as an institution. Surprisingly perhaps, for an appliance so deeply woven into the fabric of British life, the Aga was invented by a Swedish physicist in 1922 and designed to burn solid fuel. Seven years later they were being imported into the UK. By 1956 the vitreous enamel finish was offered in pale blue, pale green, grey and white as well as original cream. In the following decades oil- and gas-fired models were introduced, and in 1975 an electric version went on the market. *Tom and Pat Hally/Aga-Rayburn (2)*

Lucky People! they own THERMOS

BRAND JUGS, JARS, FLASKS

"HALF an hour spent like this," said the girl who lived by (and sometimes talked to) herself, "means that when I come home tonight there'll be hot supper ready for me. Goodness knows what time that wretched committee will finish. But it doesn't matter to Thermos, for this will be ready when I'm ready, and nothing gets spoiled if I'm late."

And what a comfort it is to be able to rely on Thermos, waiting to welcome you after a long day. What a time-saver Thermos is, too, in the morning . . . ready with porridge and breakfast coffee, prepared the night before, but piping hot now when you want them.

Unfortunately, more people are asking for Thermos goods than we can supply. So, from time to time there may be shortages. But keep asking. You'll always know a true Thermos model by the registered trade mark— and that's your guarantee of quality.

SPECIAL 'THERMOS' REFILL SERVICE

If you have the bad luck to break the glass lining of a 'Thermos' vacuum vessel, don't throw away any of the components. Consult your retail supplier on the question of fitting a new vacuum refill.

THERMOS

REGISTERED TRADE MARK
VACUUM VESSELS

Left Before the days of automatic oven timers and the microwave revolution, working women had to rely on other quick and convenient methods of preparing meals. This advertisement for Thermos from about 1952 suggests cooking supper in the morning and keeping it hot for about 10 hours in the vacuum flask! Time could also be saved by preparing porridge and coffee at night, ready for an instant breakfast the next day!

Microwave ovens developed as a result of radar experiments during the Second World War. They cook by means of very high frequency radio waves, which heat food quickly, and were introduced in the early 1960s, initially aimed at the catering market. Early demonstrations showed how several plates of pre-cooked egg and bacon could be stacked up in this revolutionary oven, reheated in a matter of minutes and emerge as though freshly cooked. All basic stuff today, but impressively modern at the time!

A domestic microwave went on the market some ten years later at a cost of around £300. Even by the early 1980s, microwave cooking was in its infancy and needed to be fully explained to the public. The fact that this 1980/1 Creda model (*above*) was a specialised product at the time is reflected in the £289.99 price tag.

Microwave ovens are a prime example of how prices drop as new and luxury appliances become everyday necessities. In 1994 66 per cent of households owned one, and this wide demand has brought costs tumbling - a basic microwave can now be bought for under £100.

In recent years, progressive features have been introduced. This 1996 AEG Micromat Combi (*below*) offers more than just a quick and convenient way to heat a meal. It incorporates a fan oven and grill, either of which can be used in the conventional way or combined with the microwave facility to give traditional cooking results in half the time. There is a pre-programme memory, allowing you to store up to three of the most frequently used cooking tasks, which can then be activated at the touch of a button. And if your meal is ready but you are not, the oven also features a 'heat and hold' facility that will keep food warm for up to 15 minutes after cooking has ended.
Rejectamenta/AEG Domestic Appliances

STRONGEST & SAFEST

The NEW "VILLA" FRENCH FRIED POTATO CUTTER

In the 1940s and '50s the average housewife relied on little more than a set of weighing scales, measuring spoons, jug, mixing bowls, rolling-pin, wooden spoon, knives and saucepans (*right*). Preparation of food was time-consuming because everything was made from scratch. Even the most proficient cook spent hours in the kitchen preparing and cooking family meals.

Small gadgets like the famous Villa potato chipper flooded the market; this 1948 advertisement (*left*) illustrates the glamorous, happy women-in-love-with-housework image that was typical at the time. Household management books of the era stressed that housewives should try to find enjoyment in their daily grind and look smart while doing it.

Today's cook still relies on the basic essentials but is more likely to use electrical gadgets. This latest Kenwood Chef (*below right*) can liquidise, mince, slice, peel, shred, sieve and grind, as well as make sausages and ice-cream. *Rejectamenta/Kenwood Ltd*

Below left and right A range of electric kettles from the mid-1960s. Materials included chromium-plated copper and polished aluminium with plastic handles, and they were priced at between £5 and £6. The automatic switch-off kettle dates from 1955, although other warnings to indicate when the water was boiling, such as whistles, buzzers and flashing lights, were on the market before this time.

Kettle design changed little in post-war years until the 1980s when the jug kettle arrived on the market. Recent innovations include cordless models, lockable lids, water-level indicators and filters that prevent limescale being poured into the drink. *Gardiner's Homecare, Bristol/MB*

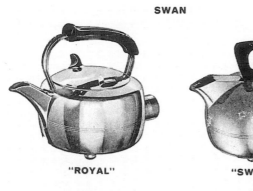

SWAN

"ROYAL"

"SWIFT"

"SIREN" WHISTLING KETTLE

"POPULAR"

PHILIPS filterline

SCONES * CAKES
PASTRY * PUDDINGS

Rejectamenta

Belling Appliances Ltd

In the 1950s no self-respecting housewife would be seen dead in her kitchen without wearing an apron, often frilly and flowery and referred to as a 'pinny'. And no housewife worth her salt would be without a home-made cake, tucked away in a tin, either for her family or in case friends dropped in for tea. Her ambition, at least according to the advertisers, was to be a perfect cake-maker, and recipe books were distributed in their millions by manufacturers of home baking ingredients. Blue and white striped Cornishware, from mixing bowls and jugs to rolling pins and storage jars, was enormously popular. Embossed biscuit-coloured earthenware bowls were also commonly seen in kitchens at the time.

A tailored butcher's apron is what today's housewife wears, if indeed she wears an apron at all. Cornishware is increasingly seen in antique shops and markets, and one dealer tells me that he can't get enough of it. Together with the big heavy earthenware mixing bowls, its revival is thought to be due to the desire for period-style kitchens. Women today report that making a cake is an occasional event rather than a daily chore.

'It's something I enjoy once in a while,' admits one. 'I do it because I want to and not because I have to. Let's face it, although there are some good commercially prepared cakes on the market, nothing really beats the home-made version.'

Bread making has also enjoyed a revival. 'I find it a therapeutic job on a wet Sunday afternoon,' says another housewife. 'And it's a wonderful treat to eat chunks, fresh from the oven, with jam and cream.'

GOOD HOME BAKING is something to be proud of

The woman who can cook well and bake well has every reason and every right to be proud of her cooking.

In ninety-nine cases out of a hundred she has a happy home, because good cooking means good food, and good food means good health.

There's no more pleasing sight than that of a happy family around a well-stocked tea-table, all enjoying their food; and the mother who is responsible for the good cooking, and who has prepared it with her own hands, has every right to survey the results of her culinary skill with pride and satisfaction.

From 'Be-Ro Home Recipes'

Women were usually taught to cook at an early age, first by their mothers (*below*), then later at school. Until the 1960s, when 'Women's Lib' was gathering momentum, the mother-daughter indoctrination was strong and inexorably linked to domesticity. Indeed, many girls who grew up in the 1940s and '50s look back with resentment that more help was expected from them than their brothers.

By the time women married and had a kitchen of their own (*bottom*), they were expected to possess a broad range of cooking skills that included boning meat, filleting fish, plucking, cleaning and trussing poultry and making everything from scratch, from pastry and sauces to puddings and cakes. That it was the woman's job to wait on men was generally accepted as the norm.

In the 1960s girls who had benefited alongside boys from an equal education, brought about by the 1944 Act, hit the outside world some 20 years later expecting more from life than domestic chains. 'When we married we vowed we weren't going to be a slave class,' recalls one. 'The irony was that no one seemed to tell our male counterparts not to expect their wives to wait on them hand and foot.'

Equality on the domestic scene was slow in coming, if it arrived at all. Recent social statistics reveal that eight out of ten women do all the washing and ironing and the lion's share of the cooking, even if they work full time.

'I don't want to swap roles completely,' admits one present-day housewife, 'but if we're out at work eight hours a day, we deserve some help and consideration.'

To their credit, more men than ever before now cook at least some of the time. It seemed to start with the barbecue. For some reason, men who never picked up a saucepan took delight in throwing steaks and sausages on to a grill in the garden. This progressed to the preparation of vegetables and a loose agreement that whoever was home first cooked the evening meal.

Fuelled by the proliferation of male television cooks, an ever-increasing choice of convenience foods and the socially acceptable era of Thatcher's Bachelors - the proud-to-be-successful-and-living-alone generation - men become increasingly willing to cook. Now, with sons quite used to seeing their fathers cook, and having to fend for themselves if mother works or they are away at university, the old joke about men not being able to find the cooker is likely to become a thing of the past.

Good Housekeeping

W. W. Winter, c1970

Until the early 1970s girls did cookery at school and boys did woodwork. Women who are now around the age of 50 would have studied 'domestic science' at school. Wearing starched white cotton aprons (provided by their parents), they were taught how to clean poultry and fillet fish and how to make Russian fish pie, apple dumplings and custard (with eggs, not powder in a tin). Correct procedure was taught in table-laying and the care and cleaning of kitchen materials. At the end of each cookery lesson, pupils were expected to scrub their wooden tables for 10 minutes with hot water and washing soda. No bacteria dared resist their onslaught!

In the mid-1960s domestic science became known as 'home economics', then about five years ago it switched yet again to 'food technology'.

There was a time in the 'progressive' 1980s when youngsters were leaving school with little or no knowledge of basic cooking skills or what constituted a healthy diet. But today 'technology' is compulsory and covers several practical subjects of which 'food' is an optional choice.

'We've been through the *Blue Peter* stage of designer sandwiches,' says a present-day teacher. 'There is a swing back to traditional ideas with emphasis on nutrition, quality-finished products and the basic use of kitchen equipment. Skills are still important.' But today pupils wear white nylon aprons (no starching or laborious ironing) and kitchen tables are wipe-clean plastic!

STORK WIVES REPORTING—ONE OF A SERIES

"My Mother-in-Law was delighted"

says newly-wed Mrs. Jane Jenkins of Carshalton

When my mother-in-law came to visit us in our brand-new house we'd only been married for a couple of months. Dick's mother is a wonderful cook, and I was just a bit nervous at first, because I didn't want to let Dick down by my cooking. But I needn't have worried! She was delighted with everything, and before she left she asked me for the recipe for my Fly-away Fancies. I told her I'd made them with Stork, because I'd discovered how wonderfully easy it makes creaming and rubbing-in. "Well, this Stork certainly makes them *taste* delicious," she said, "Thanks for the tip, Jane—I can see I'm going to become a Stork fan myself from now on!"

This is the recipe that Mrs. Jenkins gave her mother-in-law:

Having left school armed with a good grounding in domestic science in the 1950s, the greatest compliment was to be praised for your feather-light sponge, especially if it came from your mother-in-law! Few, if any, housewives dared admit to using one of the new packet cake mixes. Manufacturers knew this and advertisements used phrases like 'oven freshness' and 'home-baked taste' in an attempt to alleviate any guilt.

The 1950s was an era of extreme sexism. It was a time when cooking, and in particular cake-making, seemed to symbolise the perfect woman. Just look at the kisses you received for using Viota cake mixes. One for the large cake, another for the 18 buns, and yet a third for the cup cakes, iced in hubby's favourite flavour!

Finally, no well-stocked larder was complete without its bottled fruit. Post-war housewives spent much of their time preserving produce when it was cheap and plentiful, to tide the household over the lean winter months.

This photograph from the early 1950s (*above*) shows whole, sliced and pureed tomatoes being bottled in Kilner jars. Both jars and contents were sterilised by being placed in a low oven for about an hour. Hot syrup was then poured in and the jars fitted with a rubber seal and a glass or metal lid. To ensure the contents remained in good condition, the utensils had to be spotlessly clean and the jars perfectly sealed.

During the war, the Women's Institute set up fruit-preserving centres all over the country to deal with gluts of home-grown fruit.

Although Kilner jars are still available for a small proportion of people who like to bottle fruit and vegetables, today the more likely method of preserving food is by freezing. In this photograph (*below*) a glut of home-grown carrots is being preparing for the freezer. They will be blanched in boiling water before being packed into special freezer bags. Today many people buy 'pick your own' fruit and vegetables from farms when produce is at its most plentiful - and therefore cheapest - then freeze it for the lean times ahead.

4. EATING

In 50 years we have seen the demise and virtual extinction of the traditional way of eating. For the first 20 or so post-war years, the evening meal and mother's home cooking was the focus of family life. Three square meals served at the same time each day, together with the woe-betide-you-if-you're-late attitude was a social ritual. Serving food punctually was very important to housewives, and the expectation that all the family should be there was the basis of good manners.

Prior to the Second World War most people ate all their meals at home, with working men and schoolchildren usually returning for lunch. When women were involved in the war effort, and away at work themselves for long hours, the Government introduced school meals, works canteens and state-sponsored restaurants.

The habit of eating a midday meal outside the home continued after the war, much to the relief of overburdened housewives who were beginning to demand a life of their own. Gradually more households were able to afford labour-saving appliances and convenience foods, and women found that they had time on their hands. They turned to leisure activities or returned to work, which meant that meal times became less rigid as new-found freedom was fitted into the family routine.

In the early 1960s another phenomenon occurred which changed our eating habits for ever. The young embraced the Great American Dream, a world of coffee bars, frothy coffee in glass cups, milkshakes, elaborate sundaes and the Wimpy Bar. Here you could eat something called a hamburger (which was actually made with beef) - with your hands, no less, and in public too - without feeling ill-mannered.

Opposite page Much blamed for a decline in social standards is television. Advertisements of the early 1950s show father and children gathered around the set watching a programme, while mother waltzes in with loaded trays and frilly apron, thanking her lucky stars that she can rely on sliced bread and instant coffee and not miss 'the show'!

Food manufacturers were quick to introduce the television dinner - a mediocre offering arranged on compartmented plates, rather like the type served on airlines. Although popular with children, they never really caught on.

Books and magazines also leapt on to the bandwagon, suggesting buffet-style 'eats' that could be consumed in front of the TV without the need for knives and forks. Indeed, television brought a tidal wave of wondrous inventions to suit the newly adopted lifestyle. This TV tray from about 1955 (*opposite above*) was typical. *Both Rejectamenta*

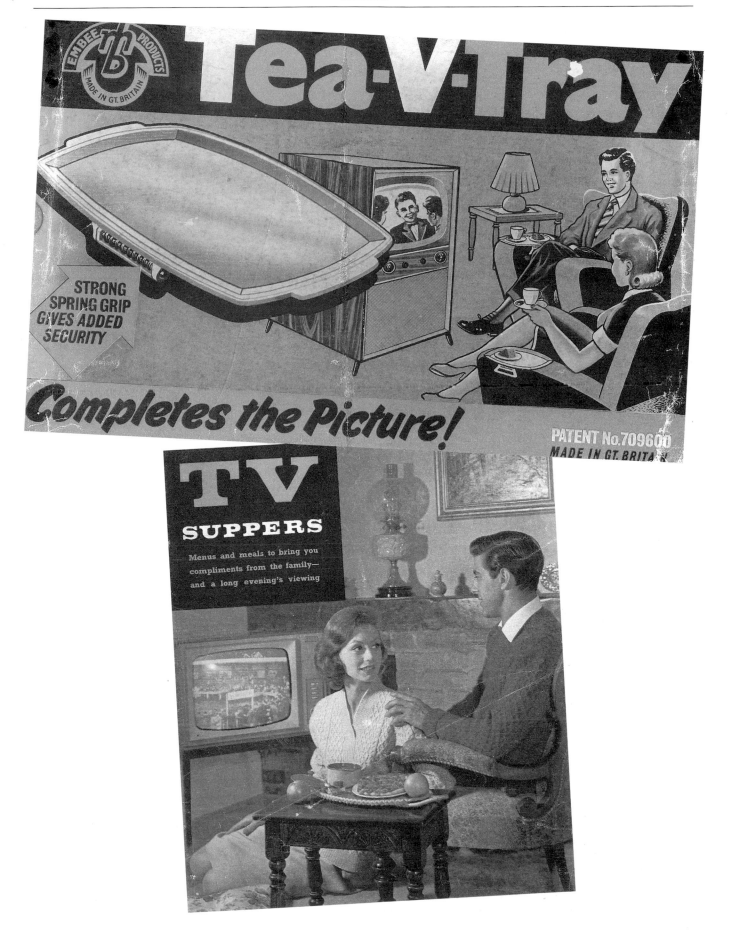

No longer does traditional family life revolve around three meals a day. Today's families are more likely to have one meal and several 'snacks'. Meal times are planned round hobbies, social engagements, work and television programmes. Often individual members eat at different times, only coming together for a family meal once or twice a week. Lap meals in front of the 'box', and the use of freezer-to-table foods are no longer regarded as the mark of a lazy or slovenly housewife.

One 50-year-old recalls, 'I'd been brought up under the strict three-meals-a-day, elbows-off-the-table regime. In the mid-1970s when my husband worked erratic hours and the children were at home, we seemed to eat in shifts, even on the hoof. There'd be homework going on at one end of the table, me eating at the other and the 14-year-old with supper on her lap watching the television. Then my husband arrived home and ate in solitary confinement.

'If he was really late he'd get a frozen roast beef platter from the freezer and microwave it. I used to feel terribly guilty until I realised that half the population was doing the same. When my mother visited I'd make a supreme effort to lay the table properly and get everyone to eat together. I felt I had to give the impression that we always behaved like that because she expected it. I was exhausted for weeks afterwards!'

In the picture above actor Rodney Bewes advertises frozen sliced meat for Birds Eye in 1975. *Birds Eye Walls Ltd*

c1951

As Sundays have tended to become less distinguishable from any other day of the week, so that great stronghold of family mealtimes - Sunday lunch - has slipped out of fashion in many households. The crunch came in the 1960s when grown-up daughters reviewed the formal eating contract imposed on them as children and rejected it.

'I remember Sunday lunch with horror,' says one. 'Mother slaved all morning peeling, steaming, roasting and stirring. I used to nag her to eat early because I wanted to meet my friends. Dad never arrived on time because he played golf on Sunday mornings. By the time we sat at the table it was often well past two o'clock. Mother was a nervous wreck and the atmosphere was poisonous.

'Now, even over 30 years later, I can't say Sunday Lunch without a feeling of panic.'

Sunday lunch was regarded as the best meal of the week. So deeply entrenched was the ritual that a certain shame arose if families couldn't afford a joint of meat. One victim recalls, 'Dad sharpened the carving knife outside on Sundays to make our neighbours think we were having a roast. But all we lads got was half a sausage each!'

Although many families still look forward to Sunday lunch - perhaps the only meal of the week eaten together - it is not a rigid ritual to be adhered to at all costs. Stuffed peppers are just as likely to be on the menu as roast beef and all the trimmings.

'Brunch' is a relatively recently coined word. A cross between breakfast and lunch, it has become a popular choice for Sundays. It gives the working wife the chance of a leisurely morning without all the rush and bustle associated with weekdays. Sunday is also often a day for going out, and together with today's high percentage of car ownership and reasonably priced pub food, lunch out is a regular event for many.

1966

Leaving home to share a flat or bedsit in London was the ultimate stab at freedom for many girls in the 1960s. Whereas in previous decades young singles were clucked at and cosseted by over-protective landladies, Miss Swinging Sixties went it alone.

'We wanted to throw off the domestic shackles endured by our mothers,' explains one. 'We weren't interested in meat and two veg, it was all oregano and garlic, parmesan and pasta. We practically lived on spaghetti bolognese, usually thrown together by the light from chianti bottles heavily encrusted with dripping candle wax. If we felt lazy, we'd just cook a boil-in-the-bag Vesta curry.

'Foreign food was all the rage in the '60s and the art of eating real spaghetti - not that tinned stuff we had at home - was the most sought after skill of the time. We'd practice for hours winding spaghetti round a fork, against the bowl of a spoon, before we dared eat it in public. We thought we were the most sophisticated beings ever to exist.'

Moving from home to a bedsit or flat is still the first real strike at independence for most youngsters today. Not only is the desire to swap warmth and comfort for damp, cold and grot common-place, but so too is sharing with the opposite sex. Mixed houses have become as socially acceptable as jeans and tee-shirts. What and how youngsters cook is just as mixed. Reports range from Cup-a-Soup to roast chicken and all the trimmings, and from Pot Noodles to the best of Delia Smith. The local pizza delivery service remains a favourite choice for a financial blow-out and, according to our 1996 picture, so does a 'liquid lunch'!

The popularity of foreign food began in the 1960s when more people were travelling abroad and eating out at the new Indian, Chinese and Continental restaurants. Spaghetti Bolognese epitomised the new taste! Heinz advertised it as 'Italian-style spaghetti' and the cans carried a picture of a well recognised Italian landmark. Batchelors' Vesta curries were also popular. These boil-in-the-bag offerings were about the only ready-prepared meal at the time that was aimed at single people.

c1959

1966; Gardiner's Homecare, Bristol

1996; Smallbone of Devizes

The kitchen-diner was a very '60s concept and one that originated in America. It was a popular idea among young couples, as another liberating influence from the rather formal dining restrictions imposed on them as children. However, snobbishness still existed among certain members of the older generation who considered that it was just 'not done' to eat in the kitchen, an attitude that perhaps harked back to pre-war days when only servants ate there. Nonetheless, trendy housewives were inviting friends to eat in their new kitchen-diners and, in tune with the times, were cooking food with a Mediterranean flavour and serving bottles of red wine.

Also, the young Swinging Sixties wife didn't want to work in isolation as her mother had done, thus missing the conversation and clink of glasses emanating from another room. In many homes the dining room was increasingly being seen as redundant - what was the point of keeping a room just for eating? Kitchens became rooms for family as well as guests, rather than the housewife's lonely domain.

Eating also became more relaxed, and young housewives of the time cold-shouldered stiff ostentatious dinner parties staged to impress hubby's boss. There was a new affluence among the young and they were eager for new tastes and cultures.

The 1970s ushered in smaller kitchens and the arrangement known as the 'lounge-diner'. Often this was an L-shaped room, the dining section of which was situated in the short leg of the 'L'. Its popularity was, however, short-lived, and the 1980s saw a resurgence towards the kitchen becoming the heart of the house.

The modern kitchen is a place where all the family congregate, cocooned in its cosy warmth. Friends are entertained there too, the conversation flowing as freely as wine or coffee. Comforting and reassuring, this kitchen is a practical place to work, yet attractive enough for the smartest dinner party.

Left In the 1950s the housewife reigned supreme; dinner and cocktail parties were the high point of socialising. With more food becoming available, housewives were expected to dish up interesting and attractive meals usually aimed at impressing her friends, her husband and his boss. Her highest accolade was when she was praised for her efforts and talked about for her good taste. It was the era when business entertaining was done at home, and career success was won or lost on the housewife's prowess as a cook-hostess. It was important that she looked the part - seen and not heard! Women's magazines of the time featured a wealth of patterns for hostess outfits, boasting such details as décolleté necklines and waists swathed in cummerbunds.

Right and below Commercially prepared food is the agent of a social revolution, designed to meet the modern housewife's view that there are far more interesting things to do in life than stand in the kitchen all day.

The range of convenience foods in the 1940s was largely limited to a selection of cans. There were also delicatessens, but these tended to be expensive and therefore not patronised by the average housewife. A limited choice of frozen foods was available, but again were considered a luxury and few housewives had storage facilities for frozen food anyway. Sliced bread and a can of Batchelors peas were about as far as Mrs Average went in her pursuit of convenience foods. Manufacturers went to great lengths to convey canned and packaged foods as a modern convenience, not aimed at independent or working women, but at the housewife hostess. Advertisements of the period left no doubt that a woman's place was in the home. This was the era when a good cook symbolised the perfect wife and it was in the kitchen where she spent much of her time lovingly cooking to please her husband. They usually featured glamorous women in a housewife's role, suggested that canned foods were useful for rustling up a last-minute meal for hubby's unexpected business guests, and the time saved in cooking could be spent on looking lovely to greet them!

Lovely creamed potato -

As much or as little as you like—
in a flash with

POM ONE-MINUTE POTATO

A big dish of nourishing Creamed Potato? Or just a little to top a shepherd's pie? You can make either in a flash with 'POM' One-Minute Potato. So easy! So quick! So delicious! Once you've used 'POM' you'll never be without it.

Try POM for these too!
CHIPS • POTATO CAKES • RISSOLES
FISHCAKES • BATTERS • THICKENING
SOUPS STEWS & GRAVIES

c1950; Reckitt & Colman Products Ltd

Daddy *will* be pleased

Don't tell him – just watch his face when you spoon a thick, generous helping of Nestlé's Cream over his favourite blackberry and apple pie. Cream that crowns and completes fruits, jellies, pies or puddings.
Pure, glorious, country cream. Nestlé's Cream.

NESTLÉ'S CREAM PURE STERILISED

Pure Country Cream with the Nestlé's name behind it

c1958

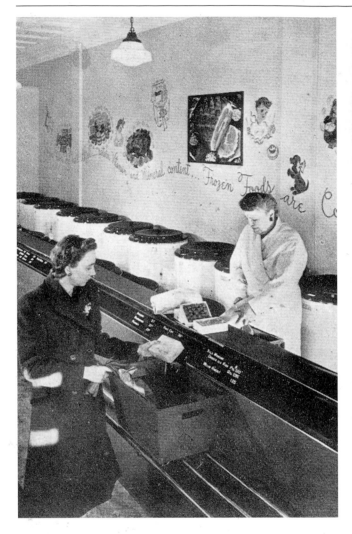

This 1947 photograph shows an American frozen food market at the time when British housewives were in the grip of post-war austerity. The caption reads: 'The picture shows an American "food mart" at which frozen foods only are sold: it is one of a very considerable chain. While frozen foods are unlikely ever to be sold on this scale in Britain, it is fairly certain that they will become a much more general feature of our town life.'

Today you only have to look round a frozen food centre such as Iceland to see cabinet after cabinet stacked with an astonish-ing range of frozen products to realise how the market has expanded. By the late 1980s the frozen food market was growing at twice the rate of the rest of the packaged grocery market, with ready-prepared meals proving particularly popular. Moreover, no longer are country dwellers deprived. Improved transportation, sophisticated communication, more car owners and the growth of home freezer ownership mean that those living in rural areas can obtain sufficient frozen provisions to last several months.

Right Although frozen food had been around since the late 1930s, few housewives were familiar with it. Even with the establishment of Birds Eye shops in the 1950s, and with more convenience foods becoming available, frozen products remained largely a luxury to be bought by wealthy people who enjoyed eating foods out of season. In 1961 Birds Eye produced just 60 lines, with peas, beefburgers and fish fingers being the mainstay; in 1995 their range comprised some 205 different frozen foods ranging from economy burgers and beef stew to steak in red wine sauce and chicken makhanwala. *Birds Eye Walls Ltd*

"Always something wonderful for every meal!"

THAT'S why thousands of housewives regularly buy Birds Eye quick-frozen foods. There's such a lot of wonderful things to choose from! Everything from fresh vegetables to delicious home-bake pies, from sea-fresh fish to a variety of poultry and meats. There's fruit and pastries, too! Wonderful eating, wonderful value, wonderful variety—all you want at just one stop, when you . . .

stop at your Birds Eye Shop

Birds Eye Steaklets—the new meat treat! You'll love the flavour—fresh, tender beef prepared as only Birds Eye know how. All ready to fry or grill!

Birds Eye Pies—full of flavour! Freshly made to bake at home. Chicken, Turkey, Steak & Kidney.

BIRDS EYE shop

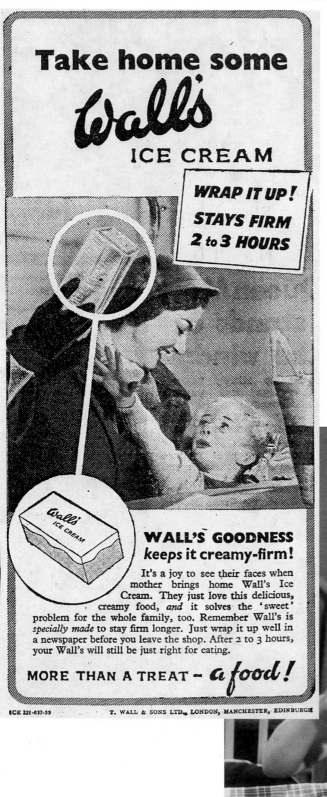

Left Ready-bought ice-cream is so much part of our lives that it is hardly regarded as a convenience food. In this 1952 advertisement it is interesting to note that sales are aimed at immediate eating - few housewives owned a fridge, far less a freezer, and ice was something that covered the roads in winter!

Making ice-cream used to be an arduous task. At college in the early 1960s we were taught how to make it when ice was not available. A freezing mixture was made by pounding together sulphate of soda, muriate of ammonia, nitrate of potash and water! The ice-cream ingredients were whisked by hand in a small bowl, which stood in the freezing mixture. It was a horrible job and your arm ached!

Right As far as children were concerned, frozen fish, baked beans and chips were in 1965 (when this Birds Eye ad was made) what McDonald's is today. *Birds Eye Walls Ltd*

As more married women worked and the ownership of home freezers grew, so the convenience food market rose to meet demand. Ownership of microwaves has more recently created further expansion, especially in the freezer-to-table market, an increasing proportion of which is aimed at the busy one-person household - complete meals on a plate that can be taken from the freezer, put in the microwave and served in a matter of minutes, without even the need for washing up. Even children, whose mothers work, can feed themselves by this method.

It could be argued that the meteoric rise of convenience foods has done more to get women out of the kitchen and into the office than any equal rights legislation! Today's housewife doesn't even have to grate cheese or chop an onion - it's all there on the supermarket shelves neatly bagged. Not only have convenience foods offered women freedom from the slog of preparing and cooking, but they are also to some extent responsible for making cooking easier and more tempting to men.

'Feeding the family seven days a week used to be a thankless task,' reports one 80-year-old. 'You'd spend hours making everything from scratch, then the family shovelled it down without a thought as to the labour involved. You were also shackled by the constraints of seasonal availability.

'But I can't believe that there are young women today who don't know how to make pastry. And when I see basic ready-made products like bread and butter pudding and beef stew all boxed up with a glossy photograph, and price tag to match, I think people must have money to burn. And all that plastic and paper packaging - what a waste of natural resources! Good old fashioned practical skills have vanished.'

From a Flavel cookery book

Afternoon tea used to be a classic daily ritual, a ceremony that lasted about an hour, and one for which Britain is famous. 'Let's have afternoon tea,' mimic American tourists in their best attempt at an upper-crust British accent.

As seen in this photograph from the early 1950s, time and thought went into table setting and the choice of china and food. Daintiness was the byword. Prettily decorated bone china, sometimes a silver teaset, damask napkins, wafer-thin sandwiches, delicate cakes and scones with home-made jam, all set out on a crochet-edged or cutwork tablecloth - often worked by the housewife herself. Sometimes crumpets were toasted on a long fork on the fire and cakes served on a tiered stand.

Afternoon tea tended to be a rather formal affair where etiquette reigned supreme. Occasionally I'd go to a friend's house for tea. As a special treat we'd have what her family called a 'Reading Tea' - we'd all have a book and read while we were eating. It was frightfully *avant garde* for the 1950s!

Today (*inset*) 'afternoon tea' is likely to served in mugs (with a biscuit if you're lucky) and consumed standing in the kitchen or enjoyed over a natter in front of a hastily lit gas fire! The art and formality of traditional afternoon tea may have vanished, but today tastes in tea are more sophisticated and you might offer friends a choice of Earl Grey, Lapsang Souchong, Darjeeling or one of the many popular herbal teas like orange blossom, mint or camomile.

'A NICE CUP OF TEA. . .'

'Tea' and 'Britain' have been relentlessly linked for centuries. Offering someone a 'cuppa' is like a national salve. In moments of celebration, crisis or chaos, the drink most of us turn to is a comforting cup of tea.

- As a nation we drink 196 million cups of tea per day.

- Tea corners 45 per cent of the beverage market.

- In the 1660s, tax was levied on tea at a staggering 5 shillings per pound.

- Until well into the 19th century tea was a valuable and expensive commodity and was kept locked in a caddy. The poor bought used leaves for a few pennies from well-off families.

- In 1717 Thomas Twining dealt an early blow for equal rights by opening a tea shop in London solely for ladies. It was 15 years later before both sexes and all classes were able to drink tea together in public.

- Glaswegian Sir Thomas Lyon first brought tea to the masses and was paramount in developing that revolutionary product - the teabag.

- 'Typhoo' is the Chinese word for 'doctor'.

- 'PG' is said to stand for 'Pre-Gestee'.

- The ancient Chinese used tea for everything from digestive problems to failing eyesight and loss of memory.

- Reputed to be the most expensive tea in the world is Formosa Oolong at £28 per pound.

- Tea-tasters enjoy a language all their own using words like 'bright', 'brisk', 'neat' and 'chesty' to describe the quality of various teas.

- Mrs Beaton tested the quality of tea by throwing a pinch into the fire, claiming that the bluer the flame the better the tea.

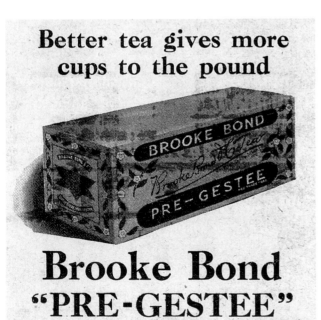

Better tea gives more cups to the pound

Brooke Bond "PRE-GESTEE"
smooth to the palate

Brooke Bond are using the finer teas they are now getting to improve their most popular blends.

Ask for "Pre-gestee," in the familiar grey packet. Your dealer will do his best to supply you.

HAWKINS "CLASSIC" LGH.5000

HAWKINS "TECAL" LGH.4000

HAWKINS "TIFFEE" LGH.1700

Early tea-makers were advertised as invisible servants for housewives who were without help in the house. The Hawkins 'Tiffee' featured in this 1965/6 advert not only provided tea every morning right at your bedside (no more dressing-gown trips to a cold kitchen), but it was also relied on for a handy cuppa while watching television (no need to interrupt your favourite programme!). The 'Tiffee' cost £3 19s 6d. *Gardiner's Homecare, Bristol*

Breakfast Menus

This breakfast, featured in a Flavel cookbook of 1962 (*left*), consists of stewed prunes, baked eggs in sausagemeat, toast and marmalade with butter curls and coffee. Smoked haddock and kidneys were other popular breakfast fare. Porridge was frequently on the menu in our house - the type made with proper oatmeal and a dash of salt, then served with thick creamy milk, not that transparent watery stuff you get today!

Housekeeping books of the 1940s and '50s suggested laying an attractive breakfast table using 'your splashiest floral china, your grapefruit glasses polished until they gleam and bright red and white place mats'!

A proper sit-down-with-the family cooked breakfast used to be a national institution but, like other traditional British meals, it is now largely a thing of the past, relegated perhaps to a once-a-week lazy Sunday morning.

At the same time as the old-style breakfast slid into decline, so the idea of eating in the kitchen sounded more sensible. Thus the 'breakfast bar' was born. It saved time in the mornings - food, crockery and cutlery were close to hand and no elaborate table settings were necessary.

Although medical experts wax lyrical over the importance of breakfast, for the vast majority today it is a rushed affair - a bowl of cereal, rolls or toast and a cup of tea or coffee, often eaten 'on the hoof' while anxiously glancing at the clock. Or worse, a service station pasty hastily nibbled at traffic lights on the way to work!

The alfresco variant of 'keeping house', a family picnic reflects the basic sanity of simple and fundamental pleasures in the early 1950s. It was the era of the Great Day Out. Families flocked to the seaside or into the countryside by train, charabanc or car, replete with sandwiches, Primus and tartan rug.

Even travelling a few miles was considered a major expedition. Day trips were planned well in advance. What would you wear? What would you take? What would the weather be like? (Some things never change!) And, oh yes, don't forget to turn off the gas and electricity and lock the door!

Sadly everything is so commercialised today that we expect to have to pay for most of our pleasures. Seaside resorts, stately homes and other day-trip attractions are having to offer bigger thrills and excitement to woo visitors. Children are caught up in a frantic age of hard-edged technology, and if you suggested taking a 10-year-old on a picnic, he'd probably reply, 'That's boring' - racing around in a go-kart, an hour in an amusement arcade followed by lunch at McDonald's would be more his scene!

Picnicking itself has also become more sophisticated. Today there are designated sites set aside in coastal and country areas that provide car parking, benches and tables and, in some cases, barbecues.

5. CLEANING

The morning routine for this young housewife of 1952 begins at 6.30 am. She is dressed for the times - neat hair, smart dress and shoes and frilly apron. Her dusting mop has a flexible handle enabling the lower half to reach under furniture. She does a daily dusting, often with a dusting glove, and runs a carpet sweeper over the rugs.

Special once-a-week cleaning includes polishing the furniture and using her Dustette vacuum cleaner on the rugs. Floor polishing takes up a lot of her time, but she plans to treat her linoleum with a liquid plastic floor dressing, which has recently appeared on the market, then all it will need is a wipe with a wet mop.

She cleans her gas cooker daily, and once a month soaks the parts in hot water and washing soda and scrubs the pipes and burners with a long-handled phosphor-bronze brush. It is likely that she uses a barrier cream to protect her hands. Before going to bed she plumps the cushions and empties the ashtrays.

Her present-day counterpart wears the current 'uniform' - jeans, tee-shirt and bare feet! She cleans her home when she feels like it or when she can't stand the mess any longer! If she needs to protect her hands, she wears rubber gloves. A duster hangs from her pocket, her vacuum cleaner boasts a range of attachments for reaching into inaccessible places, and a multi-purpose spray cleaner is used for everything, from her heat-proof and damp-proof furniture to sinks and kitchen surfaces. Her modern gas cooker has no cumbersome pipes and burners. She uses a cream cleaner or scouring pad to remove tough burnt-on stains. And there are no ash trays to empty in her house because smoking is banned!

'We seem more content to live with a bit of good honest dirt, and if we put off cleaning until tomorrow, so what? It's not the end of the world,' says Jean Hadden. 'I think we're probably more slovenly today, but I wouldn't want to turn the clock back 50 years.'

THE DAILY ROUND

This was a suggested daily routine for a couple with one child and no maid in the 1950s. The final word of the day makes one smile!

6.30 am	Rise.
6.45 am	Make bed and air room; attend to boiler. Wash and dress child; prepare breakfast.
7.45 am	Serve breakfast.
8.15 am	Clear away dishes and wash up; attend to entrances.
8.45 am	Daily washing for child.
9.15 am	Attend to bedrooms, bathroom and lavatory.
9.45 am	Dining room, lounge and hall.
10.30 am	Cook midday meal and prepare for supper. Sweep and clean kitchen.
11.40 am	Special work such as weekly window cleaning, washing paintwork, polishing floors and furniture.
12.45 pm	Complete preparations and serve lunch for self and child.
1.30 pm	Clear away and wash up; tidy kitchen; wash and change. During afternoon attend to child, shopping, mending, gardening, etc.
4.30 pm	Prepare and serve tea; feed child.
5.00 pm	Finish preparations for evening meal; lay table.
5.30 pm	Play time with child.
6.00 pm	Bath child and put to bed.
7.00 pm	Serve evening meal.
7.30 pm	Clear away and wash up; darning, patching, sewing. Recreation.

Information courtesy of Good Housekeeping Institute

GET THE *Best*

OUT OF YOUR GAS COOKER

Your gas cooker is a good and faithful servant, but it will appreciate a little care and attention. Here are some hints on how to keep it in good working order.

clean the burners

Brush the burners with a stiff brush — a good stiff brush. Clean out the holes with a pipe cleaner or a handy hairpin.

wash the grill

The grill should be taken out occasionally and given a good wash in hot soapy water.

wipe the oven

After roasting, wipe the walls of the oven while still warm to remove any grease. Once a week take out the shelves and wash them.

small gas bill

Your cooker is at its best when the oven and other parts are kept clean. It will cook better, look better and, what is more, burn less gas.

Take care of your cooker — and use gas wisely — in your own and the Nation's interest.

—— ISSUED BY THE GAS COUNCIL ——

In the 1940s and '50s housewives invariably wore a scarf tied round the head turban-style and a frilly apron or floral overall.

'We young wives were always putting curlers in our hair,' explains Jean Hadden. 'Turbans hid the curlers and made us feel tidy and attractive if we had to answer the door during the day. We'd take them out about 10 minutes before our husbands returned from work, then in they went again at bedtime.'

Jean's attitude epitomised what was expected of housewives at the time. Good Housekeeping's *Handy Home* of 1948 stated: 'She should give her husband what he needs after a day's work by providing the comfort and peace of a home and by making herself look dainty and attractive'!

'A high standard of housekeeping was expected in those days,' adds Jean. 'Cleaning was taken so seriously. We had a routine that was strictly adhered to. There were also loads of books and magazines on the market that explained how to do simple chores in fine detail.'

The steady introduction of labour-saving appliances and modern materials has had a great effect on the average

housewife's workload, relieving her of much of the daily grind and enabling her to combine a career with running a home. Changing attitudes have also affected the amount of time that today's housewife spends on cleaning her home.

'Let's face it, there are far more interesting things to do in life,' says one. 'As long as my kitchen floor is clean, then psychologically I feel that the whole house is clean.'

'With me it's the loos and sinks,' says another.

Today few women stick to a strict routine and fewer still would consult a textbook to find out how to clean a cupboard door. They just get some proprietary cleaner and a cloth and do it. Like in between making coffee and *News at Ten*!

GIVE HER A BRIGHTER, EASIER
NEW YEAR IN THE HOME
with this Christmas gift set of Addis Brushes

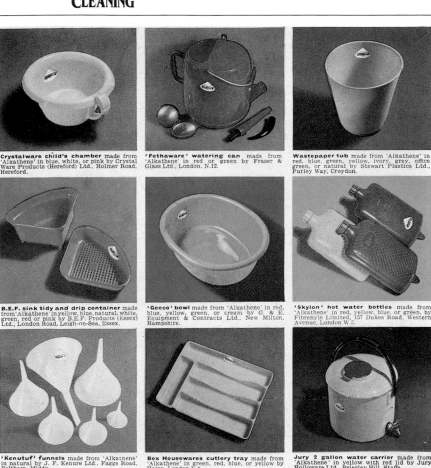

Crystalware child's chamber made from 'Alkathene' in blue, white, or pink by Crystal Ware Products (Hereford) Ltd., Holmer Road, Hereford.

'Fethaware' watering can made from 'Alkathene' in red or green by Fraser & Glass Ltd., London, N.12.

Wastepaper tub made from 'Alkathene' in red, blue, green, yellow, ivory, grey, office green, or natural by Stewart Plastics Ltd., Purley Way, Croydon.

B.E.F. sink tidy and drip container made from 'Alkathene' in yellow, blue, natural, white, green, red or pink by B.E.F. Products (Essex) Ltd., London Road, Leigh-on-Sea, Essex.

'Geeco' bowl made from 'Alkathene' in red, blue, yellow, green, or cream by G. & E. Equipment & Contracts Ltd., New Milton, Hampshire.

'Skylon' hot water bottles made from 'Alkathene' in red, yellow, blue, or green, by Fibrenyle Limited, 157 Dukes Road, Western Avenue, London W.3.

'Kenutuf' funnels made from 'Alkathene' in natural by J. F. Kenure Ltd., Faggs Road, Feltham, Middx.

Bex Housewares cutlery tray made from 'Alkathene' in green, red, blue, or yellow by Halex, London E.4.

Jury 2 gallon water carrier made from 'Alkathene' in yellow with red lid by Jury Holloware Ltd., Brierley Hill, Staffs

Above Plastic kitchenware was all the rage in the 1950s. Indeed, it was so desirable that housewives were thrilled to receive special gift sets for Christmas!

Addis, now a household name, built its reputation in the post-war years by making toothbrushes. In 1952, during the early years of plastic moulding, the company entered the domestic hardware market. Addis's first product was a novel washing-up brush with a plastic handle and nylon bristles. Wholesalers were slow to accept this revolutionary aid, but now, over 40 years later, few kitchens are without one.

Like other manufacturers of the time, Addis was a pioneer in introducing colour to the home. Director Robert Addis recalls, 'Research to find out what the housewife wanted was non-existent in those days. What went on sale was what the manufacturer decided. Housewives could therefore choose any colour as long as it was red, blue, yellow or green! When a competitor dared to introduce orange in 1970, panic broke out!'

Addis responded by making breadbins, buckets, bowls and laundry baskets in rather garish orange and turquoise. Towards the end of the 1970s dark colours like brown and navy blue became fashionable. A decade later, popularity shifted to pastels. Although red comes and goes in the fashion stakes, it remains a fairly constant favourite for kitchens. *Addis Ltd*

Addis Ltd

Top right These kitchen products of 1960 are made from 'Alkathene', which was a trade name for the polythene manufactured by ICI. The material was advertised as being tough, clean, convenient and colourful. Over the years some products have been discontinued and others introduced to meet consumer demand.

Above Although Addis remains at the forefront with its washing-up brushes, bowls and laundry baskets, items such as storage crates, large stackable boxes and waste disposal bins have become big sellers in recent years. Current favourite colours include shades of white, grey and biscuit, often with a flecked appearance.

Right The old adage 'a woman's place is in the home' certainly bore true throughout the 1950s. It was as though she had no other role in life but to scrub, wash and polish. Cleanliness really was next to Godliness! Manufacturers of cleaning products all promised the housewife easier, faster housework and a brighter home. Some advertisements were condescending, such as this 1950 example for Zebo grate polish, which says, 'How nice you feel when your husband praises the way you keep the house'!

Below Other advertisements, like this 1955 example for Parazone, portray a basic product as a valuable commodity. The housewife holds the bleach cradled in a white cloth as though it is a bottle of vintage champagne!

Rejectamenta

How NICE you feel when your husband praises the way you keep the house! If you want to feel really proud, give your grates and surrounds (and firebricks, too) the brilliant, sparkling Zebo shine. Its glistening blackness makes grates twice as warm and friendly. The whole room will look brighter, and everyone will notice the difference.

You'll find Zebo much quicker and easier to use, because it's a liquid. A rub-over and a quick polish, and you're through.

ZEBO
LIQUID GRATE POLISH
Reckitt and Sons, Hull and London

15

Reckitt & Colman Products Ltd

Above right Many advertisements of the time show women with a 'Wow, look at this' expression. They can't wait to tell other housewives how good the products are.

Right Four or five decades ago women's magazines were full of advertisements for cleaning products. Today one is likely to see upmarket perfumes, smart hatchbacks and exotic holidays, but press advertising for cleaning products has largely disappeared. Hundreds of cleaning products cram supermarket shelves, all competing for the consumer's attention. Manufacturers go to great lengths and spend enormous sums of money on package design, but the message is the same: 'Buy me'. However, in today's environmentally conscious world many say that elaborate packaging is unnecessary. With more and more people supporting 'green' issues, we may perhaps see a trend back to plainer labels and press advertising in an effort to catch the purchaser's eye.

Today we have cleaning products for every conceivable surface, including multi-sprays suitable for several uses, as well as environmentally friendly ranges.

"Cloth ears — thats' what John's got!"

"Imagine! That husband of mine buying some other cleaner when I distinctly said Vim. If he knew how much faster and smoother Vim cleans he would've *insisted* on it! Ah, well, good thing we *wives* are brighter — we *insist* on Vim!"

For smooth, fast cleaning

Brighter Wives insist on **VIM!**

Selling Agents: Hudson & Knight Limited

SO GENTLE TO MY HANDS

BROBAT Suds FOR THE BIGGEST WASH

GRAND FOR WOOLLENS SILKS AND NYLONS

ONLY 8½d FOR A 10oz. PACKET

BROBAT Suds FOR ALL CROCKERY

DOES ALL MY WEEKLY WASH

FINE FOR WASHING UP DISHES

NO COUPONS

BROBAT IMPROVED *Suds*

Both 1949

"I'm not worried about my floor, I can soon make that bright and clean again with 'Mansion'—but it's very naughty of you to take the ornaments."

MANSION POLISH
your FLOORS, FURNITURE AND LINOLEUM
Tins 10d. 1/6 and 3/9

— FOR DARK FLOORS USE DARK MANSION —

1953

In the 1950s, smart homes would probably have woodblock or parquet floors, but mortals of more modest means made do with stained floorboards or linoleum. Although electric polishers were available, Mrs Average used buckets and mops. Mansion polish was a popular floor polish of the period, while some housewives recall making their own from a mixture of paraffin and vinegar.

Makes floor polishing a pleasure!

Why polish floors the hard way when the Polywhirl 'Major' will do the work for you? Just a light to-and-fro guidance is sufficient for Polywhirl's brushes to spin and polish your lino, parquet and tiles with a lustrous finish, without effort, bending or heavy pushing.

In gay colours, complete with 'Safe-Lock' handle.

AT ALL GOOD STORES
An Amac Refinements product.
£5·5s.
GUARANTEED

Also the POLYWHIRL STANDARD, smaller than the 'Major', ideal for limited floor spaces. 63/-

THE NEW

POLYWHIRL
MAJOR
NON-ELECTRIC Rotary polisher

POLYWHIRL SAVES MONEY
— doesn't use electricity, cannot go wrong. No noise, no flex.

c1956

Right One of the most popular products was O-Cedar polish and mop, made by Prestige. The liquid polish was poured into a reservoir on the mop-head, and slowly worked its way into the cloth mop. It was advertised as 'dusts, cleans and polishes at the same time', and is remembered by many housewives as doing just that. After use the mop-head was stored in a special tin. Although the mops were discontinued some years ago, the polish has been relaunched as All Purpose Prestige Polish.

HOW WILL YOU Spring Clean YOUR FLOORS?

THE OLD FASHIONED WAY

OR THE O-CEDAR WAY

THE **O-Cedar** IMPREGNATED MOP CLEANS AS IT POLISHES

Get an O-Cedar Impregnated Mop and clean and polish your floors the modern way—without kneeling! Saves all the back-ache, and it's better for your figure, too.

Lino, parquet, stained, varnished and painted floors all come up beautifully the O-Cedar way.

The O-Cedar Impregnated Mop dusts, cleans, polishes, preserves and disinfects floor surfaces, all in one easy operation. How? Because it comes already 'impregnated' with O-Cedar Polish. To maintain the properties of the mop you stand it periodically, overnight, in its own Can into which has been added a little O-Cedar Polish. This is called refreshing the Impregnation.

The O-Cedar Mop is shaped to go into corners, hinged to worm its way into difficult places, cushioned to protect paint, etc. The pad is easily removed for washing or renewal, it will last for years. It makes floor polishing O-so-easy!

O-Cedar Impregnated Mops in special cans and with green cellulose polished metal screwed handles, from **13/3d.**

O-Cedar Polish : bottle **1/9d.**, large economy size **3/3d.**

Stocked by ironmongers, hardwaremen, stores, etc.

O-CEDAR POLISH

is the product of years of scientific study. It is an all-purpose polish excellent for furniture, paint and enamel work, glazed tiles, car bodies, etc., as well as floors. It is sweet-smelling. O-Cedar Polish collects dust without scattering it, removes dangerous dust-borne bacteria. In *one* application, O-Cedar Polish DUSTS, CLEANS, POLISHES, PRESERVES, DISINFECTS.

Above Wood floors are still very much in vogue, although now they are most likely to be sealed. One of the most common methods of cleaning them, together with painted and stripped floorboards and vinyl flooring, is with a squeezy sponge mop and a proprietary cleaner such as Flash.

Whole house heating
with **Solid Fuel**
can be yours for so little

and so easily with the help of the N.C.B. Housewarming Plan

Full central heating is becoming more and more an essential feature in the home, so long as instalments and running costs are reasonable. That's where solid fuel central heating comes into its own. No other system is so inexpensive to maintain or operate. Clean modern boilers using dust-free fuels fit attractively into your plans. Architects and Builders are quick to recognise the advantages of solid fuel central heating and can work closely with NCB fuel technologists for advice on any aspect of domestic, commercial or industrial heating by solid fuel.

c1962

Left Anyone over the age of 45 can write about cold houses! Today the comforting glow of an open fire evokes powerful images of toasted crumpets and reinstated marble mantelpieces, but 40 years ago as likely or not it meant the only source of heat. During the week a fire in the back room was your lot. On High Days and Holidays, and maybe Sundays, there was one in the front room too.

The dreaded moment came with the word 'bedtime'. You knew you had to face Arctic conditions on the stairs and in the bathroom before swapping Liberty bodice for flannelette pyjamas. Then you leapt into bed with frozen hands and even colder feet, taking your underwear with you, because - horror of horrors - you had to do it all again in the morning, in reverse!

In particularly severe winters, mother carried a shovelful of hot coals from the living room, along the hall and up the stairs to the bedroom. It was rather romantic going to sleep with flames flickering on the ceiling, even if you were wearing a cardigan, socks and unflattering hat!

Although men sometimes cleaned grates and lit fires, often it was the housewife's duty, and it was considered quite an art to do the job properly. Mother put loads of screwed up balls of newspaper in the grate, then laid sticks in a wigwam shape on top. Lastly small pieces of coal were stacked around the wood with the 'grain' running vertically. Sometimes the fire didn't take and there followed an elaborate ritual of blowing, cursing and holding up sheets of newspaper to encourage it to 'draw'. The next day the cinders were sifted through a mesh sieve and used again. The grate was black-leaded with Zebo, a popular brand of polish.

The coal merchant called regularly and it was my job to sit in the window, pretending to read, counting the sacks to ensure that mother wasn't 'done'.

This page In the 1960s central heating came of age and there was a flood of advertisements extolling its virtues. People boarded up their fireplaces, saying good riddance to the labour, grime and inconvenience. Then in the mid-1980s young couples - the original central heating generation - flocked to salvage depots in the stampede for Victorian cast iron and marble. And surprise, surprise, the open fireplace was reborn. But they had their radiators too, so the new image was a cosy focal point rather than the sole source of warmth.

Laying and lighting fires has become easier too. Firelighters and reconstituted 'logs' have done away with paper and kindling wood. Easily handled bags of smokeless fuel can be bought at petrol stations and slung in the hatchback on the way home from work.

c1954

Now **YOU** can own the best carpet sweeper ever produced

the new Ewbank

Ewbank CADET
for smaller room

Ewbank SUPERB
with removable dustpan

Ewbank ELITE

All the traditional Ewbank advantages of efficiency and sound workmanship are now given a new streamlined beauty. You will like the new Ewbank for its lighter, easy control ... smoother, silent movement ... its gentle brush action which *refreshes* the carpet pile.

MAKE SURE IT **IS** A GENUINE

Ewbank
CARPET SWEEPER

ELITE ✴ SUPERB ✴ CADET

Each in a choice of 5 gay colours

The sweeper with over 60 years of leadership

The Taylor Quads sleep undisturbed . . . because

Electrolux *Excels*

. . . in Quietness

What is the secret of the amazing *Quietness* of the Electrolux Motor ? Precision machining and special spring suspension. Thanks to this *Quietness* you can always hear the postman's knock, the telephone . . . and there's no need to switch off "Housewives' Choice" (enjoy the music while you work with the *Quiet* Electrolux).

. . . in Suction Power

The New Electrolux has deep, penetrating 'suction power, cleaning faster with gentle thoroughness, (it cannot damage pile or fabric). There are a-hundred-and-one things which the New Electrolux will clean, because it's the *complete* home cleaning system. Backed by a 2-Year-Guarantee. *Ask your Local Dealer about the Easy H.P. Terms.*

ELECTROLUX LIMITED, 153/5 REGENT STREET, LONDON, W.1.
Also Makers of Electrolux Refrigerators which excel in *Silent*, Dependable Service.

1949; Electrolux Ltd

Carpets were a luxury, and if there was one at all it was a square or rectangle surrounded by a sea of linoleum; today it would be called a rug. Electric vacuum cleaners were therefore something of a rarity, and many housewives cleaned their carpets weekly with a stiff brush and dustpan, often relying on a manual carpet sweeper, such as those made by Ewbank (*left*), for a daily 'running over'.

Note that the Electrolux vacuum cleaner advertisement (*above*) says that the machine is so quiet that 'there's no need to switch off "Housewives' Choice"'!

Spring cleaning was a common event. Dust sheets covered furniture, ornaments were removed from the room and the carpet brushed thoroughly on both sides. It was then laid out, wrong side uppermost, in the garden. Meanwhile the floorboards were checked for woodworm, then scrubbed.

Be the boss in your own home

with the new Electrolux Upright 170.

Some cleaners push you around. But not the new Electrolux 170. It does a superb job without overpowering you.

The 170 is lighter, more efficient. So you get cleaner carpets and floors with less effort and greater speed. The 170 is the cleaner cleaner. For a start, the dust-bag is enclosed in a stylish modern casing.

Secondly, a filter-pad keeps the exhaust air cleaner.

And thirdly, the disposable dust-bags just lift out – cleanly.

There's no bending to adjust knobs. The 170 adjusts itself to different carpet thicknesses. Long pile or short, the 170 automatically copes with them all. You don't even have to unwind the flex, a catch releases it for you. And a light tells you the power is on.

So give your home the new saffron and silver mist Electrolux Upright 170. And from now on – be the boss.

Price £35.17.0
(recommended)

Cost-free guarantee backed by the Electrolux nationwide service organisation.

Electrolux
UPRIGHT 170
Your obedient servant ma'am.

ELECTROLUX LTD., LUTON, BEDS.

1970; Electrolux Ltd

THE MOST POWERFUL VACUUM CLEANERS AVAILABLE

The Electrolux Airclean with its three stage Filtration System retains up to 99.99% of dust, mites and pollen where it belongs – in the bag! And now there's the choice of a cylinder model too. Start breathing cleaner air by visiting your Electrolux dealer today.

99.99% HIGH FILTRATION

Tested and Approved by THE NATIONAL POLLEN AND HAYFEVER BUREAU

FREE EXTRA PACK OF DUSTBAGS & FILTERS WITH CYLINDER CLEANER

NEW Electrolux

DONATION TO £50,000 MINIMUM DONATION TO THE NATIONAL ASTHMA CAMPAIGN (Regd Charity No.802364)

Conforms to British Standard BS5415 - the standard set for "Vacuum cleaners for hospitals and hospital or healthcare related institutions".

Electrolux Airclean Excellio
Model No. 5028
- 1400 watts ■ Low Noise
- 260 Air watts Suction Power
- Variable power control between 400 - 1400 watts ■ Combi Winder
- 'S' Class Filter ■ 9m Cord Length

SAVE £50 £199.99

Electrolux Airclean 1200 Model No. 1540
- 1200 watts Extra Suction Power
- Variable Power Control
- Stair Cleaning Hose
- Tools on board

SAVE £50 £199.99

*For an initial contract period of three years from 1st September 1995 Electrolux will donate £1 for every Airclean 1200 & Excellio (models 1540 & 5028) sold. Electrolux estimate total donations will exceed £50,000. An independent charity the National Asthma Campaign does not endorse any product and recommends you discuss any respiratory problems with your doctor.

Electrolux

Electrolux Ltd

Fitted carpets arrived on the scene in the 1960s, and by the end of the decade they were the norm and considered classy and the height of fashion. Sales of vacuum cleaners soared, and advertisements portrayed a glamorous image, hence the elegant legs and cigarette holder (*below*)!

Today's vacuum cleaners (*above*) are high-powered, super-efficient and can even remove tobacco smells and help reduce asthma attacks and allergies. Some come with a washable filter, which does away with paper bags.

BOND · WORTH

Trio

DE LUXE

This is the luxury grade of Trio – a superb modern Axminster with an extra close, deep pile. It carries the British Carpet Centre Classification 4   Suitable for heavy domestic or medium contract use.
In widths 27" and 12'.

1967; Rejectamenta

This photograph shows Model 28, the first Hoover vacuum cleaner produced after the Second World War. As early as 1919 Hoover cleaners were being sold in the UK at a cost of £25. In 1926 'positive agitation' was developed, which increased efficiency. Between 1926 and 1955 optional tools, reusable paper dags and 'dirt-finder' lamps were introduced. In the 1970s came height controls to suit different carpet piles, and in the 1980s bag check indicators and automatic flex rewind.

Recent years have seen on-board tools, autosense technology (which senses the amount of dirt in the carpet and adjusts the power accordingly), permabag and stair-cleaning systems. In the last 50 years Hoover has achieved what every manufacturer dreams of - their name becoming the generic word for vacuuming a carpet.

One of the latest designs to join our households is the friendly little vacuum cleaner with the smiling face and the name Henry printed boldly on his black hat! *Hoover European Appliance Group/MB*

Right In the 1940s it was a rare man who dared to be seen washing up! But after the Second World War the seeds were sown for a more equal partnership. Women had been used to working outside the home and men were being encouraged to take what was referred to at the time as 'an intelligent interest in domestic affairs'! Women - albeit slowly - were beginning to expect more help around the house. It has taken 50 years for those seeds to germinate, and even now domestic equality remains a figment of the imagination for many housewives!

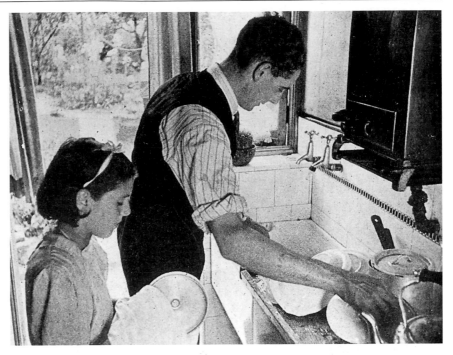

Below In 1948 Lever Brothers introduced Quix, the first liquid detergent designed specifically for washing up. It was joined eight years later by Sqezy, the first plastic squeezable bottle that we know today.
Lever Brothers

Below Surprisingly perhaps, in spite of the fact that washing up is the chore that many women hate most, 1994 statistics showed that only 19 per cent of households owned a dishwasher. This means that 81 per cent still washed up by hand! According to statistics it takes 1 hour 8 minutes to do the job manually, and 10 minutes by machine!

Now...the new DOWSING Domestic Dish-Washer

Dowsing's

See its many special features at Stand 47

★ **Fully Automatic**—Everything automatic by switch control, filling, washing, rinsing, emptying. Hands never touch water. Fills from hot water tap if available, or heats from cold if necessary. Thermostatically controlled.

★ **Washes Everything**—Cutlery, crockery **and saucepans**. After washing and rinsing, hygienically with scalding water, both dishes and dish-washer dry in their own heat—dishes ready to put away.

★ **Portable**—on castors—no plumbing or installation charges necessary. Filled and emptied from same orifice by means of adjustable tube fitting under any tap for filling, and emptying into the sink.

★ **Safe Action**—Washes by pressure only—water forced both upwards and downwards through revolving sprays. Wire tray takes all cutlery, crockery and saucepans—patented knife box protects handles.

★ **Capacity**—Two tanks, washing and rinsing—combined capacity, two to three gallons—2 kw. immersion heater in main tank, 1 kw. in rinsing.

★ **Finish**—Inside white vitreous enamel, outside cream stove-enamel.

★ **Dimensions**—External dimensions, Height 2ft. 9 ins. Depth 2 ft. Width 2ft.

DOWSING CO (ELECTRICAL MANUFACTURERS) LTD.
KANGLEY BRIDGE RD., LOWER SYDENHAM, LONDON, S.E.26

This page Very early dishwashers were an American invention and were probably more hassle than doing the job by hand. Hot water and shredded soap were poured into the machine, then paddles were agitated by turning a handle. Finally, the machine had to be emptied manually.

Automation is far more reliable! Although dishwashers made their debut in Britain in 1937, this 1949 top-loading Dowsing model would certainly have been regarded with scepticism. The attitude prevailed for 30 years, and even today, with dishwashers boasting all manner of features and carrying an average price of around £400, they are considered something of a luxury. *South Western Electricity Historical Association/Electrolux Ltd*

THE NEW AQUALUX DISHWASHER

Aqualux ESF611
Dishwasher
● 12 Place settings
● 4 Programmes
  – Economy
  – Quick Wash
  – Rinse & Hold
  – Normal
● On/off push button
● 65° Wash temperature
● Quiet – just 63 dB(A)
● Permasafe Water Safety System
● Programme progress indicator
● 850 mm (h) x 595 mm (w) x 600 mm (d)

THE DIRECT SPRAY DISHWASHER

Direct Spray ESF620
Dishwasher
● 12 Place settings
● 5 Programmes
● 2 Temperatures – 55° economy wash
                  – 65° normal wash
● Quiet – just 59 dB(A)
● Quick Wash
● Heavy Soil
● Economy Wash
● Rinse & Hold
● Residual heat drying
● Child Safe door lock
● Permasafe Water Safety System
● Adjustable Upper Basket
● 850 mm (h) x 600 mm (w) x 600 mm (d)

Opposite page The inter-war years saw considerable advancement in dishwasher design, but even in the early 1960s, when this Kenwood model went on the market at a cost of 73 guineas (£76 13s), less than 1 per cent of households owned such an appliance. *Kenwood Ltd*

"Don't worry about the washing up . . .

there's a Dishmaster in <u>our</u> kitchen!"

You really *can* forget about the washing up —when you've a Fully Automatic Dishmaster! This new machine by Kenwood does it *all* for you—in minutes! Saves your hands, too—you never put them in water!

Only Dishmaster has <u>all</u> these advantages!

- **works at one touch of a switch.** Set it—and forget it!
- **washes, double-rinses and power-dries** everything—from finest glass and china to greasy pots and pans*
- **prevents breakages.** Dishmaster's exclusive "STERA-SURGE" action means *only the water* moves, building up from fine spray to cleansing surge
- **saves hot water.** Built-in heater boosts *just the right amount* of water for perfect washing
- **is more hygienic.** Does away with germ-harbouring dish-cloths and tea towels (saves aprons, too!)
- **cleans and dries itself** as it operates
- **is so economical.** Gives *a lifetime free from washing up* for running costs of about 1s. a week.

Own a Fully Automatic Dishmaster for £23.10.6 down

and 24 monthly payments of £4.6.3 (cash price 112 gns., tax paid). Standard Model 73 gns., tax paid: with Heater 92 gns., tax paid. **Best results are obtained by using* *special Dishmaster Conditioner (dish-washing powder)*

FULLY AUTOMATIC

Dishmaster

BY *Kenwood* YOUR SERVANT IN THE KITCHEN

- -

Write to us today for free literature and the name of your local dealer

NAME ....

ADDRESS ....

....G.H.13

KENWOOD MANUFACTURING (WOKING) LIMITED · OLD WOKING · SURREY

It is interesting to note that in 1961, in an effort to boost sales, Electrolux is offering a full demonstration in the housewife's own home. *Electrolux Ltd*

Now every family can afford to
**WASH-UP
THE MODERN
WAY!**

ELECTROLUX *Dishmaid*
at 60 guineas

You've always wanted to get rid of the washing-up—now you can! For only 60 gns., you can buy an Electrolux Dishmaid—the lowest-priced washing-up machine in the country. The Dishmaid leaves your washing-up sparkling clean, dried and stored out of sight in less time than it takes to enjoy a cup of coffee. It goes on the draining-board, work-top or on the wall. Built by Electrolux for years of service, the Dishmaid takes the washing-up off your hands for good. See it today!

No fixed plumbing—operates on any normal hot water supply. Exclusive flow-rinse action ensures clean water for every wash and rinse. Powerful jets spray hot water from all angles. Unique rotating dish-rack ensures jets thoroughly clean each article. 12 months' labour-free guarantee backed by Electrolux Service Organization. Free demonstration—in your own home without obligation.

H.P. Terms £12.12.0 and 36 monthly payments of £1.17.0 or by arrangement with your dealer or Electricity Board Showroom. Wall bracket or special stand optional extra £1.15.0.

See also the full Electrolux range of refrigerators, cleaners and floor polishers at the Modern Homes Exhibition, Kelvin Hall.

Electricity Pavilion	Stand 18	Avenues E & P	M.R.S. Lanarkshire	
Superbe Electrics	Stand 15	Avenue E	H. & H. Glasgow	Stand 102 Avenue L & M
Superbe Electrics	Stand 43	Avenues J & K	John Paton, Ayrshire	

In goes the washing-up... Now your time's your own! Powerful jets spray from every angle and there's clean water for every rinse.

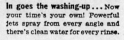

Everything clean, dry, out of sight ... The Dishmaid stores your clean dishes hygienically away, ready for use.

Electrolux
ELECTROLUX LTD., 153/5 REGENT ST., LONDON W.1.

One Year's Expenditure for Family of Four (Two Adults, Two Children), One Nurse-Housekeeper

Total income £762 after payment of Income Tax. Own house, bought in 1941 for £2,000

	£	s.	d.
Schedule A	23	5	0
Rates	24	15	0
Water Rate	2	18	0
Property insurance	4	18	0
Coal, coke and anthracite	24	8	9
Electricity	8	2	6
Gas	15	15	4
Telephone	8	9	10
School fees for elder child	12	12	0
Doctor's fees	15	4	6
Dentist	4	3	9
Chemist	6	8	0
Papers and periodicals	5	6	0
Nurse's wages (£2 10s. weekly)	130	0	0
Laundry and cleaner's bills	16	0	0
Butcher	13	0	0
Baker	8	15	0
Milk	30	0	0
Groceries and greengroceries	61	18	0
Travelling expenses, lunches, etc. (both husband and wife working)	215	16	0
Clothes	82	5	9
Total	**£714**	**1**	**5**

The general assumption that a woman's place was in the home meant that she was almost entirely dependant on her husband. It was therefore common for the wife to receive 'housekeeping' - a certain amount of money each week to buy food, cleaning materials and pay for services like laundry.

Household management books placed great importance on careful budgeting, and housewives were urged to keep meticulous records of outgoings in a special book. This is a typical example from 1948. *Good Housekeeping*

6. LAUNDRY

Various theories have been suggested over the years as to why the household laundry was always done on Mondays. One reason is that at the turn of the century poor families only had one set of 'best' clothes, which were worn on Sundays. As the labour and time involved in washing and drying was so enormous, housewives needed the whole week to complete the job.

Another theory is that women were ready to face the onerous task having been fortified by Sunday lunch (maybe their only decent meal of the week) and had enjoyed a day of relative ease compared to the rest of the week. Whatever the reason, down through the years Monday seems to have stuck, and even today there are housewives who stick to the traditional routine.

A good deep sink and plenty of hot water were considered the most important requirements when it came to home laundry. The next essential item was a wash boiler, especially for washing sheets, towels, blankets and tablecloths. Less than half the population used the services of a commercial laundry.

Wash boilers, powered by gas, electricity or coal, kept items boiling for as long as necessary. Some models came with paddles that slotted in and were turned by hand to agitate the clothes, much like the action of early washing machines. A tap was incorporated in the side for emptying the water. The c1940 example illustrated here cost only £1; in the 1950s they cost between £6 and £17, still a vast difference from the powered washing machines that were on the market at the time.

Surprisingly perhaps, it was as late as the early 1970s before sales of wash boilers declined. Over the following couple of decades washing machines gradually became more commonplace, although many housewives stuck steadfastly to their old wash boilers.

Joan Lynes recalls using her copper wash boiler for years. 'One leg fell off and I propped it up with a stick. It was worn out really but I didn't have anything else until 1983 when I bought a Bendix automatic washing machine.'

During the war householders were issued with small lidded bins in which to put waste food for pigs, but many housewives report having used them for boiling small items like pants and handkerchiefs. Yet others recall using their wash boilers for fruit and vegetable bottling.

With the introduction of easy-care fabrics, boiling died out. Nylon came first and was made into stockings, underwear, blouses, dresses and shirts. Then came Terylene, which was completely drip-dry, while the later introduction of polyester revolutionised household fabrics, particularly bedding and curtains. Eventually came poly-cotton as we know it today, beloved by housewives for its easy laundering qualities.

1956; Rejectamenta

95

The new wonder gadget of 1939 was this Super Oxford wringer (*above*). Guaranteed for 10 years and built to last a lifetime; indeed, many are still in existence, and in good working order! It would have weighed a ton, and the cost was £1, probably an average weekly wage at the time.

One 50-year-old recalls turning the handle for his mother as a boy of eight in the 1950s. 'It was a regular weekly duty for my brother and me,' he says. 'We'd lift the heavy washing out of the sink into a galvanised tin tub. Then one of us fed the washing into the wringer and the other turned the handle.

'Mother was very particular about folding the sheets and tablecloths properly. We boys held each end, pulling the four corners taut. If we let go, all hell broke loose!'

Helen Biggs remembers near disaster when she was a girl in the 1940s. 'I was swinging on the handle of mother's big free-standing mangle when it tipped over on top of me. Mother fainted but father rushed to the rescue. Luckily there was no serious damage!' *Rejectamenta*

1945

c1940

Left In spite of the popularity of wash boilers, vast numbers of housewives did the weekly wash by hand. Some used a corrugated wood, glass or metal washboard, which stood in a tub or 'posser' of hot soapy water. The clothes were then rubbed against its ribbed surface. A washing dolly was also used; this was a wooden stool-shaped object with several legs attached to the end of a long handle. Clothes, water and soap were put into a barrel-shaped dolly tub, which had corrugated sides; the 'dolly' was moved about, pummelling and agitating the clothes, much like the action of early washing machines.

Some housewives used no washing aids at all. Dave Southall recalls how his mother washed his father's overalls. 'She spread them out in the garden, flung on a bucket of soapy water then scrubbed them with a yard brush,' he explains.

Above Early washing machines were cumbersome, heavy and expensive. Hoover led the way in post-war years by producing a more modern-looking, compact machine. It was a single-tub model with an integrated hand-turned wringer. Known as the Mark 1, it cost £31 5s and could wash a load in 4½ minutes. Sceptics of the day said that the consumer wasn't ready for anything like this, but the home laundry revolution had begun. *Hoover European Appliance Group*

In 1948 only 3.4 per cent of households had a powered washing machine. The years between 1955 and 1966 saw the biggest increase in ownership - from 17.5 to 60.1 per cent. In 1994 the figure was 91 per cent. Some early washing machines, like this gas-heated model of c1948 (*above*), were little more than glorified wash boilers. Although it incorporated a hand-turned mangle, it had to be filled and emptied manually. However, not all housewives had the benefit of electricity, and some machines, like this 1949 Servis model (*right*), were available with a petrol engine.

Dave Southall remembers his mother renting a washing machine for 2 shillings a morning in the late 1940s. 'There was a woman who ran a business from our housing estate in Hull and she delivered the machine on a hand-wheeled trolley each week.' *Good Housekeeping/South Western Electricity Historical Society*

"SERVIS," the ideal fast working, perfect washing, home laundry, is in more British homes than any other make and its superior advantages are enjoyed by thousands of housewives in 26 different countries. Such widespread distribution demands a variety of models to meet diverse conditions— one new "Servis" incorporates a water heater and another, independent of mains supply, derives its power from a small petrol engine. Whatever the model, whatever future developments in design, "Servis" will live up to its proud claim "to wash better than any other."

BRITAIN'S LEADING **Servis** ELECTRIC WASHER

Washes Cleaner—Wrings Drier

WILKINS & MITCHELL LTD. · DARLASTON · SOUTH STAFFS.

THE WORLD'S FINEST   WASHER VALUE

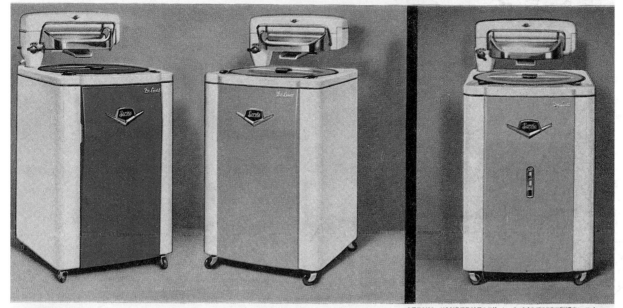

Over 30 years experience of electric washing machine manufacture goes into every machine produced in the Servis factories. The name Servis means top quality, top performance, top value for money. Servis are dependable, good looking, and up-to-the-minute in every design detail. They offer you the widest choice of models, each with the sleek, way-ahead style and efficiency you look for in today's most successful washers.

SERVIS "SUPERHEAT" is fashion-styled for today. Servis "Superheat" matches its elegant sleek lines with superb performance. "Superheat" boils the water in the tub, washes big family wash, power wrings, empties automatically. Two-tone colour combinations. £70 tax paid.

SERVIS "DE LUXE" (above left) the same superb performance but without heater. For use where hot water supply is adequate. Unbeatable value. £61 tax paid.

SERVIS "POWERGLIDE" gives you the benefits of luxury washing in compact form. Good looking and smart in performance with the power wringer that's foot controlled. This exclusive Servis feature means double safety—both hands free to steer the clothes; stop or go at the touch of a toe. Powerglide BOILS the water, washes faster, empties automatically. Two-tone colour combinations too! £54 tax paid (with heater £5.10.0 extra).

MODEL "S" The most popular manual wringer machine of all. Left- or right-hand wringer, geared for easy turning on nylon bearings, unaffected by detergents. Boils the water, washes faster, automatic emptying. £50.10.0.

SERVIS ELECTRIC WASHERS, DARLASTON, S. STAFFS • London Showrooms: 70 Park Lane, W.I

Housewives were obsessed with boiling, and many were loath to give up their faithful wash boilers, so early washing machine advertisements stressed that the appliances boiled the water. Gradually designs became more sophisticated and featured favourite kitchen colours - green, blue, red and yellow. Washing machines with powered wringers, automatic emptying and integral heaters were introduced, then came automatic fill from the house heating system and a choice of cycles to suit different fabrics.

99

Major manufacturers introduced a perforated drum rotating first one way then the other, which could be programmed to wash, rinse and spin. The front-loading automatic machine, which combined washing and spin drying, first appeared in a commercial role as DIY launderettes sprang up all over the country in the late 1950s/early '60s, fondly remembered by many young flat and bedsit dwellers as the 'coin-op'.

'It was a cheap way of spending a sociable evening,' recalls one. 'A group of us usually went on a Friday or Saturday evening to do our week's wash. We met some interesting people, formed friendships and the odd romance! Everyone chatted to everyone else, not like now when washing is just dumped in the machine with never a glance at the next person. Launderettes in the '60s were the upwardly mobile places to be seen.'

In 1960 Bendix produced one of the first fully automatic washing machines for domestic use. 'Life has never been easier' says the ad - while the machine worked housewives could relax or prepare dinner!

Today the benefits of automatic washing machines are well known. You don't even have to get your hands wet, and while the machine is working you can go off and do something more interesting than either labouring over washday or preparing dinner!

c1960

There are many, many 'matics'...

...but

ONLY ONE

HOOVERMATIC

The only 'matic' with exclusive pulsator 'boiling action'

Many to choose from? Yes! First *this-a-matic* then *that-a-matic* . . . and after you've considered the many conflicting claims, you'll probably be very confused. Relax for a moment – the solution is simple. Before you buy *any* washing machine . . . you owe it to yourself to see your Hoover dealer. Ask for a demonstration and then *compare*. Your final choice will be obvious.

Then, to the evidence of your own eyes, there's this further assurance – Hoover quality is accepted as second-to-none by housewives all over the world. Only Hoover 'know-how' gained from years of experience could produce the *Hoovermatic* – with the finest washing system money can buy. How right you'll be to choose the Hoovermatic.

With the Hoovermatic you enjoy all these advantages! ● Exclusive pulsator 'boiling action', the superlative water washing action that gives you the cleanest, quickest, and most thorough wash you have ever seen. ● Twin tubs for twice the speed . . . whilst one tub washes, the other automatically rinses and damp-dries. ● A full family wash in half an hour. ● Automatic timer . . . controls washing time for all fabrics. ● Beautiful and compact design to fit neatly into your kitchen. ● Stainless steel tub . . . cannot rust or chip.

PRICE: £79.19.5 (*tax paid*) **£85.2.7** (*tax paid — with built-in heater*).

If you judge your wash by cleanness . . . it's got to be HOOVER

With the arrival of spin dryers in 1956, wringers were dismissed as old-fashioned and a hassle to use. A year later Hoover produced a washing machine and spin dryer that fitted side by side in the same cabinet - and the famous 'twin-tub' was born.

Known as the Hoovermatic, soapy clothes were lifted manually into the spinner compartment with the aid of wooden tongs. The first lot of suds were then spun out and the spinner compartment filled with water for rinsing. After the final spin, clothes emerged damp-dry.

In 1961 came the Hoover Keymatic, a slope-fronted automatic machine, which tumbled clothes through the water rather than by the previous action of paddle agitators.

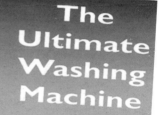

The Ultimate Washing Machine

Fifty years on and Hoover is still at the forefront in designing state-of-the-art washing machines. In the 1980s computer technology was introduced, giving reliability in use and with fewer moving parts to go wrong. With environmental concerns in mind, modern models use less water, electricity and detergent, and can save up to £49 on annual running costs. They also include components that can be recycled when the appliance is eventually scrapped. Today's consumer has a choice of ten different models, including the top-of-the-range New Wave Plus 1500, which has 50 programme combinations and retails at about £600. *Hoover Ltd*

new wave PLUS

Winner of the EC Ecolabel for Environmental Excellence

HOOVER

NEWS!

the makers of the world-famous ACME WRINGER now bring you

the ACME *Spinner*

For a drier, cleaner wash—
for a quicker, easier washday

Here is news which will bring real pleasure and satisfaction to housewives everywhere, who know and trust the great name of Acme.

Into this new Acme Spinner has gone all the wealth of skill and experience, patient research and brilliant craftsmanship, which for 80 years have made the Acme name famous throughout the world.

Now—Acme can make your washday easier, your clothes drier and cleaner, because everything you have wanted from a spinner is here—and that something more—Acme quality.

Go to your dealer today. Ask him to show you this new Acme production. You will be delighted with its beautiful finish, how easy it is to handle, and how well it will fit into your home.

How simply it works . . .

1 Just place washed clothes in Spinner. Start motor by closing automatic safety lid—and everything is ready in 3 to 4 minutes.

★ ★ ★

2 The Acme Spinner is square in shape so that it fits snugly against your sink, and has a recessed top to keep water from spilling as you put wet clothes in.

★ ★ ★

3 When everything is finished it goes neatly and compactly into any corner of your kitchen.

ACME *Spinner*

ACME—*the most famous name in washing equipment*

£29·17·6
INCLUDING PURCHASE TAX

★★★ *Ask for details from your local Electricity Board Showrooms or from a good class Domestic Equipment dealer* ★★★

ACME WRINGERS LIMITED · DAVID STREET · GLASGOW S E

c1958

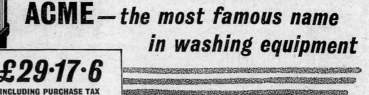

Left Spin dryers became a popular addition to the kitchen, working alongside wash boilers. Even if housewives did their laundry by hand, it was a lot less labour intensive to lift the clothes into a spinner, to extract excess water and rinse, than using a sink and mangle.

Right A selection of spin dryers on sale in 1966. After 4 minutes spinning in the Creda Debonair, clothes were ready for ironing. It cost £26 and was mounted on wheels so that it could be easily moved in and out from under the worktop. Sales of spin dryers declined as automatic washing machines became more financially attainable. *Gardiner's Homecare, Bristol*

Below Although spin dryers are still sold, the market is largely confined to flat dwellers and single households who do most of their washing by hand. The 1996 price for the Creda Debonair is £130.99.
   Christine Hughes found a novel way of using her old spin dryer - she removed the casing and grew rhubarb in the drum! *Creda Ltd*

MORPHY-RICHARDS "ASTRAL" SBU/1

CREDA "DEBONAIR" "NEW POPULAR"

CREDA "DEBONAIR" DE LUXE. SD701

A.E.G.SD25

A.E.G. SD35

"THERMAIR"

At a time when most household fabrics were made of cotton or linen, boiling was considered the best method of keeping the laundry sparkling white and hygienically fresh. Most housewives used a combination of washing soda and grated household soap; others used more modern soap powers like Persil, Rinso and Oxydol, although these were not of the standard of today's detergents. Water had to be extremely hot to be anywhere near efficient at getting clothes clean, which is probably why boiling remained so popular.

Dreft and Lux flakes were also around at the time, as well as the Co-Op's Paddy, but such products were considered luxuries and confined to hand washing silks and woollens.

After the articles had been boiled, they were hauled into the sink, often with the aid of large wooden tongs, then rinsed several times. Inadequate rinsing caused grey 'whites', and excessive use

of soap caused yellowing, and that would never do! Excess water was squeezed out by feeding the laundry through a hand-turned mangle or wringer, which was often clamped to the sink.

Soap wars

For over 100 years the two giants of the detergent industry - Lever Brothers and Proctor & Gamble - have been battling it out for the lion's share of the market, each promising the housewife a whiter, cleaner wash. Detergent sales are therefore fiercely competitive and amount to the biggest consumer product advertising budget.

Probably the best known and longest running is Persil. Launched in 1909 as the 'amazing oxygen cleaner', it took its name from its blend of PERborate and SILicate.

- 1900: introduction of soap flakes that dissolved more quickly and easily than bar soap.

- 1925: spray drying of soap powder made a more efficient product.

- 1950: first successful soapless detergents for the weekly wash became generally available in Britain. They were not made from traditional fats and alkali but from complex chemicals, many of which were obtained from mineral oils.

- 1968: introduction of biological washing powder that contained enzymes to tackle problem stains.

- 1970s: advent of automatic washing machines led to the development of low-sud powders.

- 1987: introduction of liquid laundry products.

- 1989: introduction of compact powder detergents that give superior cleaning power from only half the amount of powder (by volume) compared with conventional powder.

- 1990: introduction of compact liquids, and launch of colour-care compact powders and liquids designed specifically for colour care and protection of fabrics.

- 1996: introduction of compact powder detergents that give superior cleaning power from 25 per cent (by weight) and 40 per cent (by volume) compared with original 'ultra' powders. Cartons use over 80 per cent recycled board, and plastic bottles use 25 per cent recycled plastic.

- 1998: Persil available in tablet form.

Jenny trips up badly . . .

THE SCHOOL BELL hadn't rung yet and Jenny felt fine in her nice white frock. Washed in one of the new washing powders!

She skipped gaily on her way. . . .

And then Anne came by—in a white frock that was so *dazzling* white everyone could see the *difference* with half an eye.

As someone said: "Now, *there's* a girl whose Mum knows that *Persil washes whiter!*"

THE HIDDEN BUBBLES

Persil whiteness is simply through-and-through *cleanness*. Millions of oxygen bubbles *ease* out the dirt as nothing else can — as was proved

recently when Persil won the Good Housekeeping Institute's great Whiteness Test. Six famous washing powders were tested — and 305 out of 3? housewives voted the Pers washed tea-towel the white of all!

Yes, Persil beats the lot!

And Persil forms N SCUM, even in hard water

WOOLLENS AND COLOUREDS,

Persil cleanness brings up yo coloureds *brighter, fresh* Its gentleness keeps wooll *soft,* silks *silky!*

Yes, Persil is kind to A your wash—and to your har **You can** *feel* **it is!**

PERSIL
washes whiter!
AND THAT MEANS CLEANER!

IER 1954-436-100

You'll get loads more out of new Persil Colour big box Isn't that great news.

c1954   *Lever Brothers*

Tide makes all your Washing the WORLD'S CLEANEST...

Women who know wrote the letters below **Tide has a fan-mail** that film stars would envy. These letters from grateful housewives are typical of the thousands, glowing with praise, received by Hedley's, Newcastle upon Tyne.

SHIRTS

A letter from the Channel Islands:

"My husband has to crawl through greasy pipes, etc., to do welding jobs. Every morning he'd go to work in a clean shirt and by lunch-time it would be filthy. When I thought of all the scrubbing I'd done, I'd just let fly at him.

Then I tried Tide. Honestly, it's terrific, saves hours of scrubbing and temper. I'll never, never be without it."

PYJAMAS

A Scottish mother writes:

"I did the big family wash with Tide yesterday and find it more than lives up to the qualities described on the pack.

But what really amazed me was seeing washed-out clothes appear brighter and fresher, especially my girlie's pyjamas. My heartfelt thanks to you."

CURTAINS

From Cheshire comes this letter:

"A friend of mine was given money to buy herself a dress. She told me: 'I must get new curtains instead—the old ones won't stand washing.' So I said: 'Use Tide.'

She soaked her curtains in Tide and came back to pick up the pieces as she thought. But her curtains were beautiful, they only wanted to dance!

She calls Tide a Fairy Godmother."

HOUSEHOLD LINENS

A lady writes from Bristol:

"Having used Tide since 1951, I cannot speak too highly of it. I have been told by others what a lovely colour my household linens are, and as I am in my 80th year, I give credit to Tide—the biggest boon I have ever had."

CHILDREN'S CLOTHES

A mother writes from Prestwick:

"I began using Tide the other day and after steeping was amazed that I did not have to rub at Jennifer's dresses. She is 17 months old and gets filthy but all the marks were out. So I am going to save on her dresses—no more hard rubbing."

A HEDLEY QUALITY PRODUCT

Turn to Tide and see for yourself! See why Tide is the world's best-selling washing product!

CLEAN! CLEAN! CLEANEST WASH OF ALL!

c1953

Many soap powders have come and gone, with names long since buried in the subconscious, but while package design may have changed, and also the quality of the contents, some old faithfuls are still with us after more than 50 years of washing. *Rejectamenta*

Every housewife starched her clothes and household linen. The aim was to give the articles just the same firmness that they had when new. Starching imparted a crisp freshness and help keep the items cleaner for longer. A smooth glossy finish was achieved if fabrics were pressed when damp with a really hot iron.

Robin starch was probably the best known, and although it is now sold in spray cans, which makes the job much quicker and easier, few housewives report starching on a regular basis. 'I use spray starch occasionally on cotton blouses and shirt collars and cuffs,' says one. 'It does give a nice finish.' *Reckitt & Colman Products Ltd/ MB*

With Robin Starch aprons look crisper, stay cleaner longer

How different an apron looks after light starching with Robin! It's sparkling—fresh as a spring morning, and the sparkle lasts because Robin resists creasing and dirt.

Aprons, table-linen, bed-linen, dresses, shirts, collars and cuffs not only look far smarter with Robin, but they stay clean longer. Starching helps to prevent dirt entering the texture of materials. In the next wash the dirt simply drifts away. Robin saves rubbing, scrubbing and hard wear to the fabric. Simple, economical Robin—so easy to use, so well worth while.

ROBIN Starch
keeps things crisper, cleaner, longer

To help you starch professionally well, write for the booklet "A Little Bird Told Me" to DEPT. A2, RECKITT & SONS LTD., HULL

c1961

Below In the rock 'n' roll years, the stiffer your petticoats the more your friends envied you. One teenager of the time remembers using a sticky solution of sugar and water, which worked a treat! *Reckitt & Colman Products Ltd*

c1960

HOME LAUNDRYWORK

Plate 67

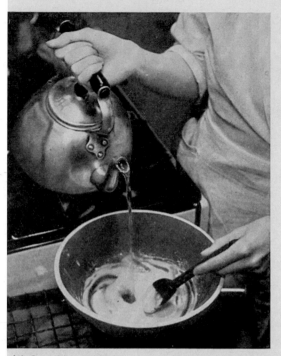

(*a*) *Starching:* add boiling water till starch 'clears'

(*b*) Rub the starch solution well into the fabric

(*c*) When using plastic starch, immerse the material when it is clean and dry

Good Housekeeping

Starch was made by mixing the fine powder with boiling water, stirring until it turned clear, then adding cold water. The squeezed-out laundry was immersed in the starch solution for a few minutes before being wrung out and hung on the line.

Many housewives made the mistake of over-starching. Marge Southall recalls, 'After my mother had finished laundering my father's bib and brace overalls, they were as stiff as boards with starch. As a girl I'd love pulling the legs and sleeves apart.'

BLUE RINSING!

How to do it

Rinsing is very important if you wish to be satisfied with your washing. Give your white things several rinses in clean, preferably soft water, wringing out between rinses to ensure that all traces of soap suds and dirt are removed. Most housewives use two or three rinses, and Blue should be used in the last of these. Do remember that Blue cannot give of its best unless white things are properly rinsed beforehand.

The correct strength of blue to use is most important, but it is not difficult to arrive at. The apparent depth of colour varies with the depth and colour of the bowl you use, but to avoid being misled by this, either of the following simple tests may be applied. These are:

(a) Let the blue water run through your hand—it should appear the very palest of sky blue, or,

(b) Dip a white breakfast cup into your blue water and match the blue in your cup with the blue in the cup illustrated on the back page of this leaflet.

If you follow either of these two methods, you should have no difficulty.

One other point to remember, keep the blue water well stirred, otherwise particles of blue will settle out on to the sides of the bowl. If your white things pick up these particles, you may get streakiness or patchiness. If you are unfortunate, and this does occur, don't be unduly alarmed. Blue is quite harmless to even the most delicate fabric, and will disappear if you put the article back into the wash.

RECKITT'S BLUE in the 'LAST RINSE'
keeps your linen a good colour!

Rinsing in Blue

1 Squeeze the bag of blue gently into the rinsing water, until the colour is evenly distributed.

2 To judge the colour strength, let the blue water run through your hand, or use a white cup as shown on the back page.

3 Dip the articles ONE AT A TIME in the Blue water, keeping them moving.

Reckitt's Bag Blue in bags ready for use. Reckitt's Paris Blue should be unwrapped and put in a flannel bag before use.

1948; Reckitt & Colman Products Ltd

'Blueing the whites' was a common method of making sure laundry was 'whiter than white' before the days of ultra-efficient detergents. Reckitt's famous little blue bag was a brand leader and was used in the final rinsing water. Many housewives fell foul of over-blueing, and many husbands went to the office wearing baby-blue underpants!

Jean Winscombe experienced even more of a disaster. 'As a teenager in the 1950s I really fancied a fashionable blue rinse on my fair hair. I found mother's blue bag in the kitchen and dabbed it on my hair. Well, I looked like something out of a circus. It never washed out and I lived with bright blue hair for weeks.'

Designed to be used in washing machines, today's Glo-white products include stain removers, super whiteners, ultrawash boosters and colour run removers, which rescue whites from mixed-wash disasters.

Washing blankets at home in 1948 meant hours of back-breaking work. Either the bulky items were kneaded and squeezed in a large sink or trampled in the bath. Dirty blankets would need two washes and several rinses before being folded and passed through a wringer.

Housewives would choose a good drying day then hang their blankets in a breezy part of the garden. A housewife's prowess as a homemaker was measured by her full line of washing drying in the garden - and oh, the shame if it wasn't as sparkling white as her neighbour's!

Where once you would have seen rows and rows of back gardens each boasting a line of billowing washing, today it is a rare sight. More and more people are relying on tumble dryers to dry their washing, although many still take advantage of a warm day when the air and sun whitens and freshens the clothes.

Rotary lines, which can be folded down and packed away when not in use, are now enormously popular. Not the case though for families on a housing estate in Bristol who, in 1995, faced a contro-versial ban from hanging out their washing. The developers, Second City Homes, insisted that the ban was necessary because drying clothes on lines looked untidy! *Good Housekeeping/MB*

Some things never change! Surprisingly perhaps, this photograph, taken as recently as 1995, shows washing hung across the street between terraced houses in Yorkshire. Families living in cramped, often gardenless, homes, especially in industrial areas of the country, have been drying clothes like this for centuries. *Chris Hughes*

IT COSTS LESS! AT THE G.U.S.!

CLOTHES RACK AND STEP LADDER

No more difficulty in drying and airing your washed clothes. With this Clothes Rack you'll need much less space and have much more spare time. Soundly constructed with four 8 ft. laths, two japanned Brackets and complete with three pulleys, cleat hook and necessary cord. This alone is worth ten shillings! But for that amount you also get a sturdy Step Ladder. Lattice type, easy-folding, with four steps. Light weight but rigidly strong.

State Number.
No. PA/3346   THE SET COMPLETE   **Carriage Paid 10'-**

10'- SET

No. PA/3346

c1940; Rejectamenta

'In bad weather you just had to dry the laundry indoors,' says Brenda Dix. 'I didn't have any fancy drying appliances, just a line in the kitchen. My son's nappies used to stink of cooking smells!'

Jean Hadden recalls, 'I hung my wet washing on a clothes horse in front of the coal fire, which caused all the windows to steam up.'

And Joan Morris had a near miss when she put her daughter's school socks under the grill to dry, and they caught fire!

Traditional pulley-operated drying racks are once again being made and proving popular in period-style kitchens.

NEW BURCO "DRIP-DRY-AIR"

NEW COTTO

HAWKINS "HI-DRY"
LGH1325

BURCO "TUMBLAIR"

Left Although drying cabinets and tumble dryers were around, few homes had them. These 1965/6 drying appliances include the Burco 'Drip-Dry-Air', which allowed a current of warm air to circulate around the clothes when the machine was switched on. Clothes were hung from an extension arm raised above the cabinet.

Another popular drying device was the Hawkins 'Hi-Dry'. The extending wooden frame was equivalent to 30 feet of clothes line, and hot air wafted upwards from an electric convector-type heater in the base. *Gardiner's Homecare, Bristol*

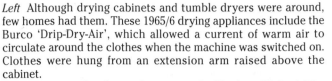

British weather *beaten* by new 'English Electric' Tumbler Dryer

AUTOMATIC DRYING FOR THE WHOLE WASH WEATHER OR NOT . . .

It's wonderful ! And it's quick ! ! Your whole wash gently *tumbled* dry in a continuous, warm, drying breeze in the corner of your kitchen ! Everything you wash the Tumbler Dryer will dry — damp dry for ironing *or* bone dry, whichever you prefer. It's so simple . . .

HERE'S ALL YOU DO . . .
Put in your wash *straight from wringing*. Set the drying time you choose on the *one-knob* control. That's all ! Your wash is gently (*so very gently*) tumbled dry. And when time's up—this marvellous Dryer automatically switches itself off ! Leave it to finish the job while you get ahead with the housework. Weather beaten—time saved. Wonderful !

SEE IT TODAY . . .
The 'ENGLISH ELECTRIC' Tumbler Dryer is being demonstrated at your local 'ENGLISH ELECTRIC' Dealer and Electricity Service Centre. Hurry along and see for yourself what everybody's calling " the greatest washday miracle ever thought of !"

'ENGLISH ELECTRIC'
BRINGING YOU ♦ BETTER LIVING

The ENGLISH ELECTRIC Co. Ltd., Domestic Appliance and Television Division, East Lancashire Road, Liverpool 10

Can be yours for as little as
£7 DEPOSIT and 14/2 per week.
Cash £69.10.0. Tax paid.

Take full advantage of this. Free yourself from drying drudgery today.

Above and right Today the most efficient and time-saving method of drying home washing is by means of a tumble dryer. Although these were on the market in the early 1950s, fewer than 1 per cent of households had one; in 1994 the figure was 41 per cent. The other 59 per cent were forced to use a launderette or a motley collection of folding airers that can be placed near a radiator.

In the days when the majority of clothes and household linen were made of natural fibres, ironing was labour intensive and time-consuming. Fabrics such as cotton, linen and silk had to be ironed when damp, and seams and embroidered parts pulled taut, otherwise you would end up with creased and puckered rags.

As long as housewives had good drying weather, they often did their washing and ironing in one day; the conscientious housewife would not want to leave piles of ironing lying about!

Early electric irons plugged into the ceiling light socket as many homes did not have power points. In 1949 a new National Service recruit recalls pressing his trousers with such an iron. 'On being called for duty I downed tools,' he explains. 'When I returned some hours later I couldn't understand why the iron was dangling a few inches off the floor. I'd forgotten to switch it off and it had burned straight through the trousers and the table!'

Electric steam irons appeared on the market around the late 1940s. Surprisingly perhaps, a cordless model was another newcomer at the time. A specially designed stand, forming part of the ironing board, provided the electrical contact necessary to heat the iron; the board was plugged into an electric socket.

However, in spite of such technological advances, many housewives were still ironing with gas or flat irons. 'I had two flat irons,' recalls Christine Morgan. 'While one was heating on the Rayburn, I'd be ironing with the other. I think there was a chrome plate that slipped over the iron to give a smooth surface for pressing. Of course there were no thermostats on flat irons. You'd touch the sole plate with a well-licked finger and if it sizzled it was hot!'

Older gas irons were heated on a gas burner, while more 'modern' models incorporated an integral burner, the gas being supplied by a flexible tube. Thermostats first appeared on electric irons in 1936.

Today, although easy-care fabrics have removed much of the sweat from ironing, there is still the temptation to stick it in a cupboard hoping that it will go away! And haven't some of us at some time dragged out our son's school shirt saying guiltily, 'Don't worry, your body heat will get the creases out'?

'I never iron everything in one go,' reports one middle-aged housewife. 'I'm more likely to dig something out of the basket and iron it when I need it.' And 24-year-old Mary Holbrook says she never irons. 'If clothes look like needing a press, I hang them in the bathroom when I'm taking a shower and the damp steamy atmosphere does the job for me,' she says.

Although some irons on the market today look surprisingly like those of the 1940s and '50s, many are almost futuristic in design. Modern irons, often in pretty pastel shades, feature non-stick sole plates, transparent water reservoirs, automatic switch-off after 30 seconds, fine mist sprays and advanced steam chambers, which prevent splodges of water leaking on to the laundry. There are also cordless irons and boards that heat at the same time, so articles can be ironed on both sides at once. *Good Housekeeping (2)/MB*

Both c1948

7. SEWING AND KNITTING

Few housewives were without a sewing machine. Although electric models had been available since 1910, many machines in use in post-war years were hand-turned or worked by pressing a treadle back and forth with the feet. Some manufacturers specialised in small electric motors to convert manual machines into electrically operated models.

Sewing machines were used for mending, dressmaking and giving a new lease of life to worn household linen. Old blankets were made into cot covers or babies' sleeping bags. If the fabric was a poor colour, it was often dyed a pretty pastel shade, then bound with satin ribbon. The best parts of tablecloths were made into smaller items like tea, trolley and tray cloths. Borders were sometimes added with rows of coloured machine stitching or hand embroidered in chain or stem stitch, which often toned with household china.

Edges of frayed towels were reinforced with bias binding or, if they were beyond repair, turned into two smaller towels or lavatory cloths. Sheets that had worn thin in the centre were cut in half, turned sides to middle and sewn back together again with as flat a seam as possible to avoid discomfort. Holes were darned and patched again and again until such time as the remains were used for patching other articles.

One present-day housewife recalls her mother's use for worn-out sheets. 'I was brought up in rural Lancashire and even in the 1950s we made our own sanitary towels. Old sheets were cut into rectangles then rolled up, tucked into a pocket and tapes sewn on the end. After use, the wretched things were washed and bleached, then used again. It wasn't that we were poor; rather, I think, because we lived in the country and access to shops was difficult.

'My mother also boiled and bleached animal feed sacks, which were made of finely woven cotton and were perfect for drying dishes. She always said that proper tea towels were useless!'

Tom Hally, who was brought up in rural Ireland, remembers sleeping between sheets made from sacking. 'Mother bought big 22-stone flour sacks from the local grocer,' he explains. 'She'd unpick the side stitching and open them out, then join two together to form one large sheet. These were boiled about four times until the sacking was really clean and soft.' Many women never lost their wartime mentality and the make-do-and-mend era lasted well into the 1960s.

Today, crafts like patchwork have become art forms, colour co-ordinated to match designer interiors, far removed from

1950; Allan Mott

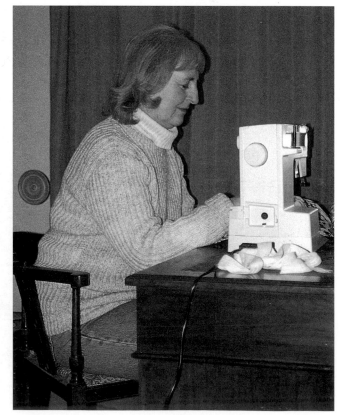

their humble origins when, born of necessity, women cut and stitched whatever oddments were to hand to make a warm bed cover. Modern sewing machines are likely to be used for such craftwork as patchwork, appliqué, quilting and elaborate embroidery, and state-of-the-art models can do just about everything except cut the fabric. Meanwhile our old (or maybe not so old) household linen ends up washing the car because, even if we can't really afford it, we like change. The wonderful choice of colours and designs on sale today are just too good to miss.

A lot has happened to the textile industry over the past 50 years. Manufacturers who survived two World Wars and the lean years in between vanished without trace in the 1970s. Lancashire-produced cotton, once a working man's fabric, is now a luxury. Vast factories, warehouses and mills that proudly clothed Britain and much of the world today stand silent and empty.

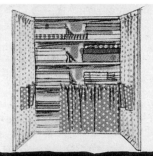

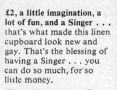

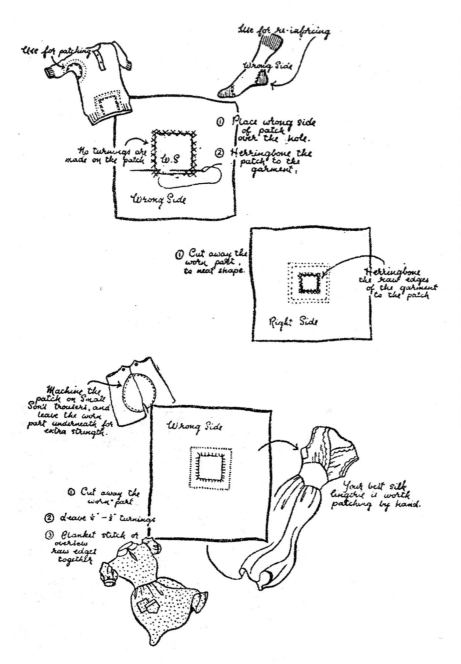

Use for patching

Use for re-inforcing

Wrong Side

No turnings are made on the patch

w.S

① Place wrong side of patch over the hole.
② Herringbone the patch to the garment.

Wrong Side

① Cut away the worn part, to neat shape.

Herringbone the raw edges of the garment to the patch

Right Side

Machine the patch on small Son's trousers, and leave the worn part underneath for extra strength.

Wrong Side

① Cut away the worn part
② Leave ¼" – ½" turnings
③ Blanket stitch or overseu raw edges together

Your best silk lingerie is worth patching by hand.

On studying his favourite torn Levis, an 18-year-old was recently heard to comment, 'I wish Grandma was still around, she was brill at mending stuff. My mum's hopeless.'

Darning and patching skills - and it is a skill to do the job properly - have all but disappeared. Housewives used to be past masters at recycling; every last scrap of wear was squeezed from clothes and household linen.

If her family was to look well groomed, and her home bright and attractive, mending must be part of the housewife's weekly routine. Some women set aside afternoons to do their sewing, perhaps putting their feet up and listening to the wireless. Others, usually mothers of large families, often stitched and picked late into the night. No housewife wanted to look slovenly in front of her friends and neighbours!

Helen Biggs of Buckinghamshire recalls long after the war wearing pyjamas that were completely made of patches. 'It was a difficult and hard life for women,' she says. 'My mother always seemed to be sewing as new clothes were almost unobtainable.'

Stockings were darned until they resembled a road map, then finally cut into pieces and used for stuffing cushions and soft toys. Interestingly, dry cleaners used to employ menders who sat in the window, professionally repairing nylon stockings.

'It is said that the rhythm of the needle, when all the difficulties of manipulation have been overcome, is as soothing to the nerves of a woman as smoking is said to be to the nerves of a man.'

'Any child who has learned to sew will gradually form a feeling of well-being. Sewing may also be the means of creating a feeling of sympathy and social service for others, for not only will the child sew for herself, but she will offer to help her mother and those whom she sees about her, who often have more than enough to do without the addition of the household sewing.'

From a pre-war school textbook

Left: *Shabby blouse made gay with collar and panel of lace.*
Right: *Tight woollen jumper becomes an attractive bolero.*

Old directoire knickers, sides turned to centre, made into new-style panties. And, right, "piece-bag" knickers made from eight small godets.

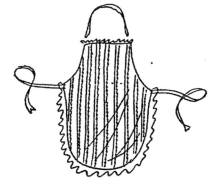

An easy conversion: old shirt-back into useful apron for housework.

Backs of worn out shirts were turned into aprons. These were gaily decorated with patch pockets, frilled hems and big bows imitating the Hungarian fashion, which was popular in the 1940s and '50s.

One friend recalls, as a boy of seven in 1952, wearing clothes made from the backs of his father's shirts. 'Mother would have already turned the collars and cuffs so that father had as much wear as possible from the shirt,' he explains. Indeed, it was common practice to meticulously unpick the tiny stitches, then turn collars and cuffs inside out so that the worn bits were concealed.

New collars and lace trimming transformed shabby blouses; woollen jumpers, which had shrunk or become too tight, were converted into boleros; unfashionable clothes were remodelled into something more up-to-date, or cut down to fit children.

Today, apart from sewing on buttons, few people bother to mend anything. We live in a throw-away society when many off-the-peg clothes and cheap foreign imports are not made to last. Today's housewife would never consider converting an old coat into a child's jacket! Our cast-offs are more likely to end up at one of the thousands of charity shops that have mushroomed in recent years.

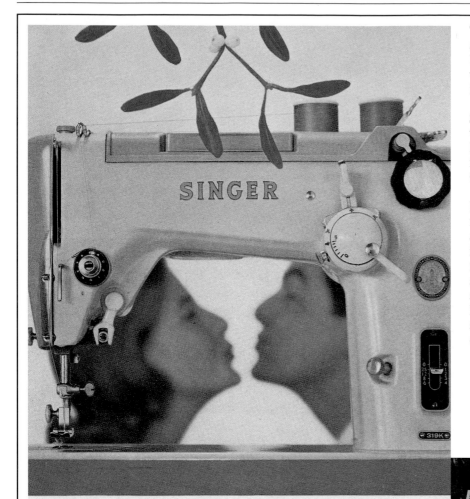

There is one name universally associated with the sewing machine business - that of Singer. Isaac Singer was an American who borrowed $40 in 1850 to make his first machine.

First manufacture of Singer Sewing Machines outside the USA was in 1867 in Glasgow; 15 years later the biggest of the Singer factories was built at nearby Clydebank.

Isaac Singer was responsible for bringing sewing machines to the masses, and his selling, marketing and advertising techniques were, for the 19th century, considered revolutionary. There was hardly a spot throughout the world that his salesmen did not reach, and in 1856 he launched a 'buy now, pay later' scheme, surely the earliest example of hire purchase.

My Husband and I are having a beautiful new Singer for Christmas

We're having a superb new Singer Automatic Swing Needle machine. One like this. He pays. I sew. We both save. The Singer Swing Needle sews everything. It darns, hems, ruffles. It embroiders, automatically, at the flick of a finger. It makes the curtains, mends the linen, makes fashion clothes for me, baby clothes (for John, when he arrives), and something extra special for *him*. After all . . . it's *his* Singer, too!

When you buy a new Singer, they teach you how to use it, how to make the most of it. And Singer easy terms suit *everyone's* pocket.
Why not sweetheart your husband into buying you a Singer for Christmas? Just lead him to the nearest Singer Sewing Centre. There's so much fun, so many lovely things to make, when you have a Singer in the family.

Christmas is fun with a SINGER
* A Trademark of THE SINGER MANUFACTURING CO.

c1959

- 1910: introduction of electric sewing machines.

- 1950: introduction of a machine that featured embroidery stitches. The cost of an average machine was £40.

- 1956: introduction of the first swing-needle machine, and manual button-holing.

- 1968: introduction of automatic button-holing.

- 1976: introduction of the first computerised machine.

In 1996 Singer's top-of-the-range computerised XL 100 model cost £2,299 and incorporates a mind-boggling range of embroidery patterns and revolutionary features. *Both Singer UK Ltd*

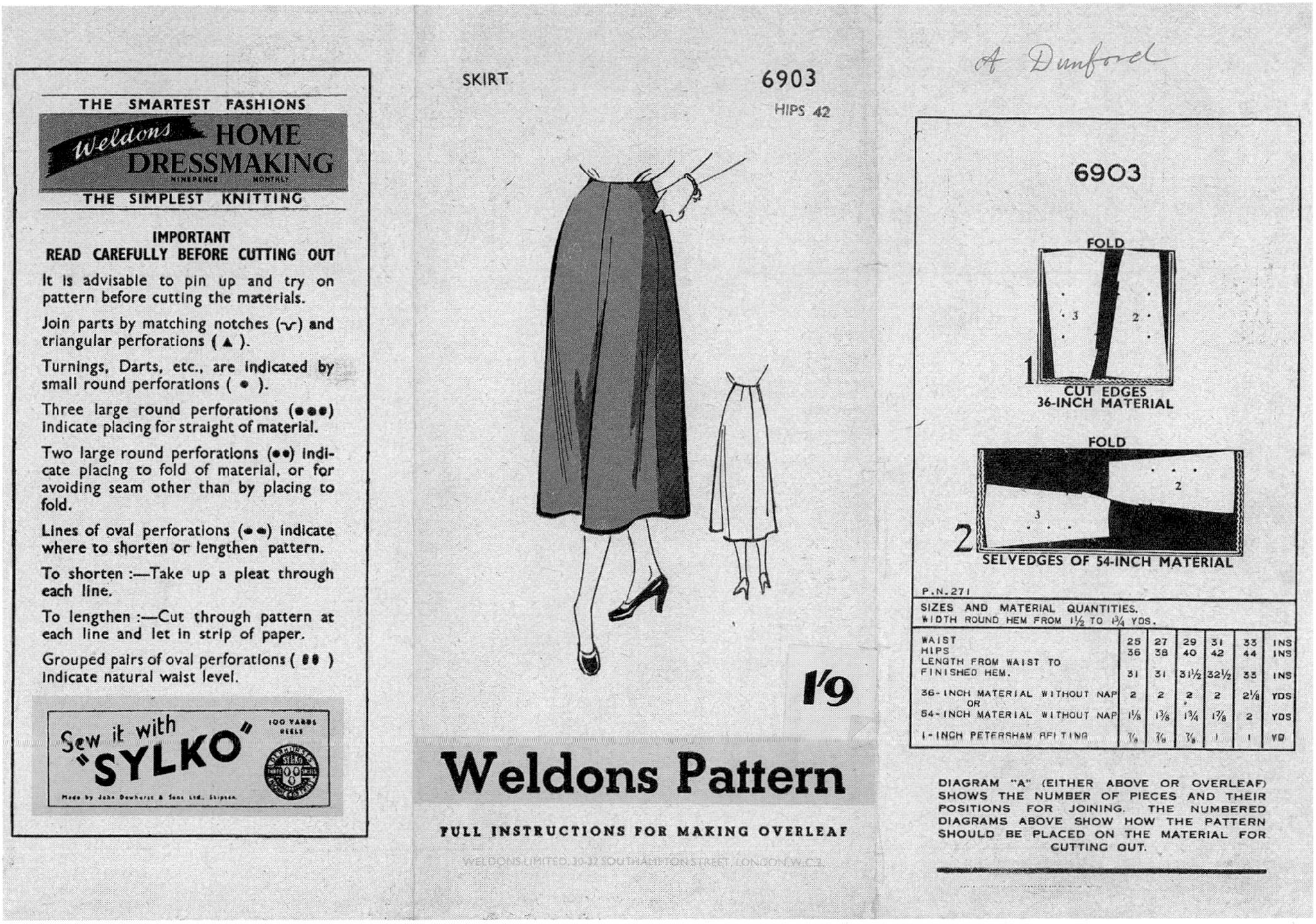
THE SMARTEST FASHIONS
Weldons HOME DRESSMAKING
NINEPENCE MONTHLY
THE SIMPLEST KNITTING
IMPORTANT
READ CAREFULLY BEFORE CUTTING OUT
It is advisable to pin up and try on pattern before cutting the materials.
Join parts by matching notches (-v-) and triangular perforations (▲).
Turnings, Darts, etc., are indicated by small round perforations (•).
Three large round perforations (•••) indicate placing for straight of material.
Two large round perforations (••) indicate placing to fold of material, or for avoiding seam other than by placing to fold.
Lines of oval perforations (••) indicate where to shorten or lengthen pattern.
To shorten :—Take up a pleat through each line.
To lengthen :—Cut through pattern at each line and let in strip of paper.
Grouped pairs of oval perforations (••) indicate natural waist level.
Sew it with "SYLKO"
100 YARDS REELS
SKIRT
6903
HIPS 42
1/9
Weldons Pattern
FULL INSTRUCTIONS FOR MAKING OVERLEAF
A Dunford
6903
FOLD
1
CUT EDGES
36-INCH MATERIAL
FOLD
2
SELVEDGES OF 54-INCH MATERIAL
P.N.271
SIZES AND MATERIAL QUANTITIES.
WIDTH ROUND HEM FROM 1½ TO 1¾ YDS.
WAIST 25 27 29 31 33 INS
HIPS 36 38 40 42 44 INS
LENGTH FROM WAIST TO FINISHED HEM. 31 31 31½ 32½ 33 INS
36-INCH MATERIAL WITHOUT NAP 2 2 2 2 2⅛ YDS
OR
54-INCH MATERIAL WITHOUT NAP 1⅛ 1⅜ 1¾ 1⅞ 2 YDS
1-INCH PETERSHAM BELTING ⅞ ⅞ ⅞ 1 1 YD
DIAGRAM "A" (EITHER ABOVE OR OVERLEAF) SHOWS THE NUMBER OF PIECES AND THEIR POSITIONS FOR JOINING. THE NUMBERED DIAGRAMS ABOVE SHOW HOW THE PATTERN SHOULD BE PLACED ON THE MATERIAL FOR CUTTING OUT.

1940s

Many women of the 1940s, '50s and '60s recall making a dress a week or running up a skirt in a weekend. It was common, too, for housewives to make quite detailed children's clothes such as shirts, trousers, swimsuits and anoraks.

During the war, when there was little choice of materials, Joan Morris remembers getting hold of a silk parachute. 'I dyed it by boiling up onion skins and flowers to produce different colours,' she explains. 'One of the things I made was a petticoat and my boyfriend was always joking about pulling my rip-cord!'

It was not until the Swinging Sixties that fashion designers aimed for the masses. There was a boom in home dressmaking: styles of the era - mini skirts, sleeveless shifts and straight dresses - were easy to make, and there was a huge explosion in paper patterns produced by firms like McCall's and Simplicity.

Towards the end of the 1970s fabrics, patterns, zips and buttons rose in price, and compared to the cost of ready-made clothing - much imported cheaply - dressmaking became less financially viable. Today this still appears to be the case, although a spokeswoman for a large department store reports that professional dressmakers seem to be making a comeback. If women don't possess sewing skills themselves, they are willing to pay to have a garment made, particularly if they have something specific in mind but can't find it in the shops.

Bridal wear is also popular with home sewers. The enormously high cost of ready-made wedding dresses offers do-it-yourselfers considerable financial savings. Elaborate and individual designs in silk and lace are possible for a fraction of the cost of off-the-peg gowns. Classic, romantic patterns are much in demand now, with styles echoing the fashions from *Pride and Prejudice* and *Gone With The Wind* proving particularly popular.

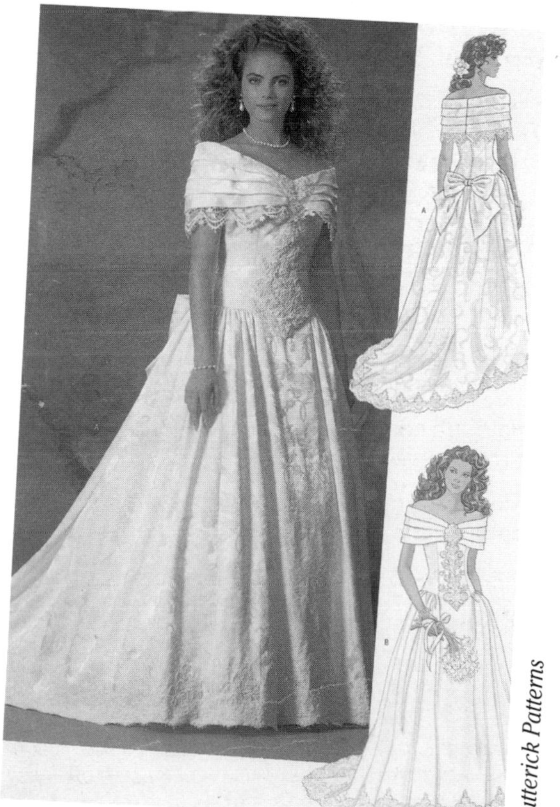

Butterick Patterns

In the early 1950s man-made fabrics appeared on the market and manufacturers widely advertised their products to tempt women to buy. Nylon was promoted as the new wonder material - labour-saving in its washing, drying and ironing qualities. Clydella, Viyella and Dayella remained firm favourites for making warm children's clothes and nightwear.

For 50 years Dylon has been a household name in home dyeing. In the 1940s, '50s and '60s clothes lines throughout the land bore witness to its popularity - everything from old woollies and odd stockings to faded bedspreads and curtains were given a colourful new identity.

The little air-sealed aluminium tin, with its powder contents, is still going strong. One teenager of the 1960s recalls, 'Stocking manufacturers had yet to realise that their limited range of anaemic shades were definitely not *de rigueur* with the sweet sixteens. But we were a resourceful lot and Dylon shares probably rocketed!

'Into a saucepan of water went the contents of the little tin and after 30 minutes simmering on the kitchen stove, the stockings emerged - a beautiful and fashionable nut-brown colour. We also stripped the colour from odd stockings, then redyed them into matching pairs.

'A few years later, as a student, I remember dyeing my dressing gown bright red in the basement laundry of our London hostel. A big sign hung on the wall saying "No Dyeing". The job was well under way and the floor was flooded with red dye. You'd think I'd murdered someone! I was beginning to panic when I heard the Irish voice of our warden coming down the corridor. As the laundry door burst open I froze. Imagine my relief when I saw my friend killing herself laughing. She was brilliant at imitating people's accents!'

Dylon is a real success story. In the early 1940s a former sculptor, artist and journalist - a Mr Gutmann - began making dyes in the garage of his London flat. He worked at night, mixing the colours in bowls, hand-filling the tins and designing all his own promotional material. Gutmann sent out samples and the orders rolled in.

In May 1946 he formed his company, Mayborn Products Ltd. Three years later he moved to larger premises in Sydenham, from where Dylon was exported around the world. At the time the

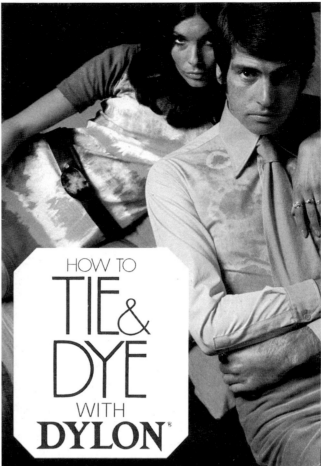

HOW TO TIE & DYE WITH DYLON®

company wondered why such big orders for black dye were arriving from West Africa. It was discovered that women were mixing the dye with oil and using it on their hair!

In the early 1950s Dylon sold for 6d per tin, and 36 colours were available, with green, navy blue and pastels proving particularly popular. At the 1952 Ideal Home Exhibition, Dylon White was introduced. This came in tablet form and was claimed to be a sensational washday discovery by making white clothes cleaner than the laundry and colours bright and new again. Dylon White came in aluminium strip form and cost 8d per pack. In the early 1970s 'tie-dyeing' was a popular craft. The effect was achieved by folding and binding the fabric, then dyeing it in one or more colours. The dye penetrated some areas of the material more than others, which resulted in highly individual patterns. This leaflet produced by Dylon in the 1970s perfectly reflects the flavour of the era.

Today a little tin of Dylon will cost you £1.60. Trends have gradually moved towards increased ease of use and reduction of effort on behalf of the home dyer. Washing machine dyes were introduced in 1989 and are now the company's fastest growing product.

Fifty years ago dyeing was an extension of the 'make do and mend' mentality. It was a quick way of bringing a new lease of life to jaded clothes. Today one retailer reports a similar trend. 'There's a boom in dyeing jeans,' he says. 'Khaki and blue are particularly popular. At £35, youngsters can't afford to chuck out the old pair and buy new just because they fancy a change of colour.'

What is new today is that dye is being used instead of paint to colour wooden furniture. But it is doubtful that anyone is using Dylon today to colour their hair! *Dylon International Ltd/MB*

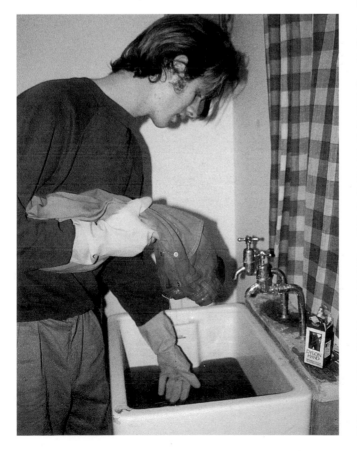

A book of knitting patterns published in the 1940s said, 'Knitting is an old and honoured craft of this country and so simple to learn that there cannot be many people who have no knowledge of its principles.' It is unlikely that this holds true today because knitting, like many other practical skills, is a dying art.

'I can never remember not being able to knit,' reports one middle-aged housewife. 'Like cooking and sewing, it was something you learned at a young age, often from your mother, then later at school. You'd start by knitting simple items like dish clothes and scarves then progress to cardigans, jumpers and socks, which were worked on four needles. It took a bit of practice turning the heel successfully.'

The choice of ready-made clothes was limited and expensive so, like dressmaking, knitting tended to be a means to an end. And together with cooking hubby's meals and ironing his shirts, knitting him a sweater was also considered an act of love!

c1952

Knit for those you love

Love someone? Then you'll love to knit for them. And the pleasure is even greater when you knit with 'Ramada'. This beautifully soft wool comes from 'Viyella House' in all the latest, loveliest colours. A special joy to use in knitting machines. Perfect for hand knitting, too. 2/- an oz.

'Ramada' REGD.
from 'Viyella House'

William Hollins & Co. Ltd., Viyella House, Nottingham. Makers of 'Ramada' Baby Wool, 'Visylka' Quickerknit, 'Royalist' Double Knitting Wool.

c1960; Rejectamenta

Until fairly recently the majority of knitting wool was sold in loosely coiled and twisted hanks, known as skeins. These had to be converted into balls before use and it needed two people to do the job. Children - boys and girls - helped mother, younger brothers and sisters helped older sisters, and friends helped friends. One person held the wool looped over outstretched hands while the other wound it into a ball. If no one was around to help, the skein was stretched over two chairs placed back to back.

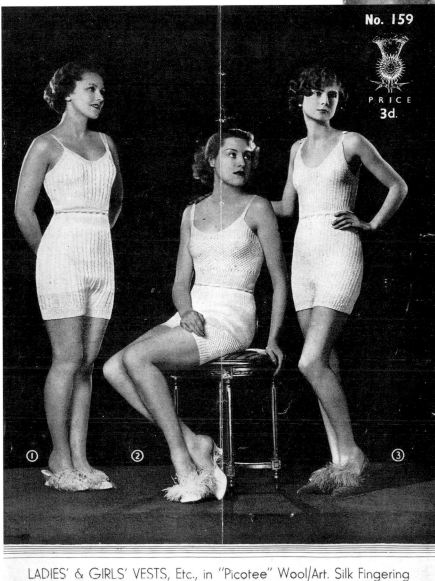

No. 159

PRICE 3d.

① ② ③

LADIES' & GIRLS' VESTS, Etc., in "Picotee" Wool/Art. Silk Fingering

JAMES TEMPLETON & SON LTD. AYR SCOTLAND

In the 1940s it was common practice to knit underwear. This typical pattern of the period was bought recently at a Bath flea market. The dealer said, 'My mother knitted the vest and pants for me last winter. They felt wonderful, warm, comfortable and strangely sexy!'

Brenda Dix remembers having to wear similar underwear during the war and she didn't find it at all sexy! 'Mother couldn't afford to buy wool so she made mine out of dish cloths. I added some gathering down the front of the vests to give them a bit of shape.'

BESTWAY
KNITWEAR
A2578
4D

POLO MODE HATS
1 or 2 ozs. 3-ply and 2 to 4 ozs.
Double Knitting

12 VARIATIONS
(see inside)

This page and opposite Women's magazines and wool manufacturers produced huge numbers of knitting patterns to suit fashions of the time. In the 1950s, every teenager (or her mother) was knitting a bobble hat of one sort or another.

In the 1960s came sleeveless mini-dresses and wrap-around jackets. Bri-nylon, a British man-made synthetic yarn, was all the rage among home knitters.

MODE HATS

No. 2   No. 3   No. 4

No. 5   No. 6   No. 7   No. 8

No. 9   No. 10   No. 11   No. 12

woman's own
Individual
KNITTING PATTERNS IN BRI-NYLON

OCTOBER 7th
EACH SHEET
EASILY
DETACHABLE

woman's own PATTERN
IN BRI-NYLON
1
*Knitting instructions
overleaf*

The image of women knitting in rural cottages enjoyed a revival in the 1980s. Chunky knits in rainbow colours and elaborate designs appeared in up-market shops. Suddenly everyone wanted a knitting machine. Even to women who had never picked up a ball of knitting wool in their lives, home knitting took on a whole new meaning. Many used their machines to earn extra income by knitting clothes for other people.

c1970: Rejectamenta

Visitors were spellbound when the new Model 305 AUTOMATIC was previewed at the London Do It Yourself Exhibition. This was the first time that the 305 AUTOMATIC had been demonstrated to the public and the reaction was fantastic. The crowds, which included many owners of Knitmaster machines were astonished at the simplicity of operation and incredible versatility of this new model which supersedes the 302 as the "maestro" of knitting machines.

Sylveia Brown, demonstrator, was overwhelmed. "We have demonstrated Knitmaster machines at all the major exhibitions but the reception of the new 305 took my breath away.

People just stormed on to the stand to see the new machine. I think the word must have got round that we had something special on show because people – men *and* women – seemed to be coming straight to the stand without paying much attention to other exhibitors. Saturday was just fantastic, we had to place up extra staff to cope with the rush".

What's all the fuss about?

– It's about the most staggering development in home knitting machines this century!

Send today for an advance copy of our colour brochure describing the new 305 AUTOMATIC.

1970s machine knitting

Today there is such a choice of ready-made knitted garments, most reasonably priced, that hand knitting has become less financially viable. Today's housewife is more likely to knit as a hobby. The clicking of the needles and seeing something useful take shape is both therapeutic and satisfying.

DLC

INDEX